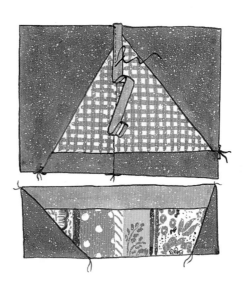

patchwork

patchwork

projects · techniques · motifs

Diane Crawford

Text by Lucinda Ganderton

Photography by Linda Burgess

RAINCOAST BOOKS

Vancouver

page 1: Sampler Rug (see page 46)
Page 2: Harlequin Quilt (see page 88)
Page 3: Mosaic Cushions (see page 28)

Illustrations • Kate Simunek

First published in Canada in 1998 by
Raincoast Books
8680 Cambie Street
Vancouver, B.C. V6P 6M9
(604) 323-7100
www.raincoast.com

First published in 1998 in U.K. by
Quadrille Publishing Ltd.

Published in association with the National Magazine Company Limited
Country Living is a trademark of the National Magazine Company Limited

Canadian Cataloguing-in-Publication Data is available from the publisher

ISBN 1-55192-216-9

Printed in Singapore

contents

Introduction

Patchwork and quilting belong to a flourishing tradition of hand craft skills. At one time, needlework was an essential element of daily life. Women made and mended garments to keep their families clothed, and stitched the bedcovers which kept them warm. Quilting, because of its scale, was often a group activity and friends and relatives would gather together to complete the final stages of making a bedcover. The quilt itself became a testimony to love and family life, symbolizing physical warmth and the shared process of creation. When you start work on your own patchwork cushion, throw or quilt, you too will become a part of this continuing history.

When we look at an antique quilt, the perspective of time lends a certain period charm to its hand stitching, the choice of design and the old-fashioned faded cotton prints. Remember however, that whatever you make today will embody its time in the same way. It will tell its own contemporary story and be completely personal to you. The ideas behind it and the decisions which went into making it will come to represent a particular part of your life. Your patchwork may well become an heirloom in the future, so when you finish a project you should embroider it with your name, and a date to record when it was made.

The process of actually piecing together and stitching takes many hours. Devote plenty of time to selecting a combination of pattern and fabrics which really appeals to you, so that you will enjoy creating the patchwork and can return to it with pleasure, again and again. It is easy to go out and buy all the fabrics you need, but the real challenge comes from using your own ingenuity to create something special and exclusive. The projects in this book incorporate scraps, fragments and offcuts of cloth from many sources, all of which bring with them their own specific memories and associations. Think of the fabrics as a basic palette and combine the colours as if you were painting with them, to make your work spontaneous and full of energy. Use the following chapters as a source of inspiration, interpret the designs in your own way and let them be a springboard for your individual creativity.

Getting started

The minimum of equipment and the simplest sewing skills are all that you need to put together a piece of patchwork. With thoughtful planning, however, and an awareness of the important role of colour and pattern, you can select a design and fabrics that reflect your own tastes and personality, and combine them to make a quilt that will become part of your life.

The following chapter introduces some of the broader aesthetic and practical aspects of quilt making, which will enable you to create a very personal interpretation of a long-standing tradition.

equipment

If you visit a quilting shop or look round the patchwork section at your local haberdashers, you may be bewildered by the amount of equipment that is available. To start off, however, you will only require the basic sewing tools that quilt makers have always used: needle, thread, pins and scissors. You will be putting a lot of time and care into your stitching, so it is well worth investing in good quality equipment and materials at the outset, to help you achieve a professional and long-lasting result.

Sewing tools

Most needleworkers will already have a workbox in which to store miscellaneous items of sewing equipment. This may be a wicker basket with a cotton draw-string lining, or a specially designed wooden box with foldout trays or several small drawers. Art storage boxes or plastic tool boxes from a hardware shop make practical containers for all the various bits and pieces that you will accumulate, and are easy to transport.

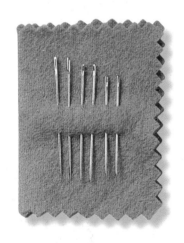

Needles

There are several types of hand needle, each used for a specific purpose. You will need three different sorts for your patchwork: ordinary sewing needles for stitching patches, short ones for quilting and longer ones for tacking. All needles are graded according to size: the higher the number, the smaller the needle will be. Finer needles enable you to produce smaller stitches. New, sharp-pointed needles are best to work with, so always discard any that become bent or blunt. Store your needles in a felt needlebook or the original packet, as they tend to get lost in a pincushion.

Needle-threaders are useful for threading needles with a small eye.

• 'Sharps' are mid-length and have a small oval eye. They are suitable for general sewing and hand piecing, and come in a range of sizes.
• 'Betweens' also have an oval eye but are shorter, so they pass easily through the layers of a quilt without bending. Choose a size between 7 and 10 to make small, neat quilting stitches.
• 'Straws' are extra-long needles, used to sew large, quick stitches and for tacking.

Protecting your fingers

If you are going to hand piece your quilt it is a good idea to get used to wearing a thimble on your sewing finger, even if you have never used one before. Choose one which fits snugly, without being too tight. A metal version with a flat, grooved or ridged top is best, as needles will slide off a domed end. Silver is traditional, but will wear through with heavy use. A lighter weight plastic thimble may prove more comfortable. A thimble is essential for hand quilting, when the extra pressure needed to push the needle through several layers of fabric can quickly give you calluses and punctures. You should also wear a second thimble or quilter's leather finger guard on your other hand to prevent damaging your nails and fingertips.

Pins

Choose long, rust-free dressmaker's pins, at least 2.5cm (1in) in length to pin the patches together before machine stitching. They should be fine enough not to leave marks on the fabric and to allow the foot to run over them without damage. Store them in a small tin or box.

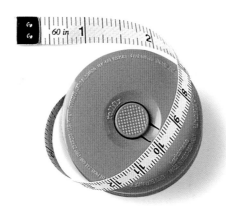

Safety pins
Pinning is a good alternative to tacking the layers together when assembling a small quilt. Special short quilter's pins, which are designed with a slight bend, are easy to use, but standard safety pins are just as effective.

Tape measure
This should be at least 152cm (60in) long, and made from a strong long-lasting material.

11

Thread

You will need different types of thread for each of the three stages involved in making a quilt:

• Tacking or overlocking thread is loosely spun from cotton and should be used for temporary stitching only. Large cheap reels can be found at haberdashers and on market stalls. Use a contrasting colour so that the stitches can be unpicked easily, but make sure that the dye is fast.

• Sewing thread comes in two types. All-purpose polyester cotton can be used for any fabric and for hand and machine stitching. 100% cotton thread is strong and has a smooth sheen. It is used especially for hand sewing and quilting.

• Quilting thread is made from cotton-coated polyester and is extra durable. It is slightly thicker than ordinary thread, which means stitches will show up more than those made with cotton thread.

Scissors

The best quality scissors have high-grade steel blades which will last many years and can be re-sharpened as necessary. Ideally you should have three pairs:

• Medium-sized cutting out scissors are easier to use than dressmaking shears when cutting patchwork pieces.

• Embroidery scissors with small pointed blades or thread clippers are useful for snipping and trimming thread.

• Paper scissors should be used only for cutting backing papers.

Sewing machine

A new sewing machine is a major purchase and modern electronic versions can perform many tasks. They are designed for making garments and soft furnishings, but as patchwork involves no more than straight seaming, only the most basic machine is necessary. Ensure that the tension is even and the stitches regular, and as with hand sewing, always use a sharp needle.

Iron

An efficient steam iron is needed to remove creases from fabric before cutting out your patchwork shapes and for pressing seams.

Drawing equipment

You will need the following selection of art and stationery supplies for charting accurate templates and cutting out the backing papers:

• Graph paper, with either a metric or an imperial grid, for drawing up squares, rectangles and 45 degree triangles.

• Isometric paper, which is printed with a network of small triangles, will save time when measuring hexagons and 60 degree triangles or diamonds.

• Pencils with a hard, sharp point (H or 2H) to give a fine precise line.

• Pair of compasses for drawing curves and circles.

• Craft knife, preferably with a lightweight handle and replaceable snap-off blade.

• Steel ruler or metal straight edge to use with the craft knife, and plastic or wooden ruler for measuring length.

• Office stapler for holding together layers of paper when cutting out templates and special remover for taking out the metal staples.

• Masking tape is used for marking lines when quilting. Look out for a low-tack tape and do not leave it stuck to the fabric for too long, or it will mark.

Patchwork and quilting equipment

You will also require a few special items to help you cut accurate fabric shapes and mark out quilting patterns. They can all be found at patchwork suppliers or craft shops.

• Rotary cutters are available in several sizes. Look out for one with a fully retractable, straight-edged blade and always cut onto a cutting mat. Only use it for cutting fabrics, and keep a spare blade, as they tend to become nicked or blunt with use.

• Cutting mats have a self-healing surface which won't dull the blades. They are printed with a grid to assist measuring and come in various sizes. If possible, buy a large one (45 x 60cm/ 18 x 24in) for cutting strips and a small one (30 x 45cm/12 x 18in) for patchwork pieces. The mats must always be stored flat or they will become misshapen.

• A quilter's ruler is an invaluable tool when used in conjunction with a rotary cutter. It is made of thick, clear perspex, marked with parallel lines for measuring strips, squares and rectangles. A large set square is also useful.

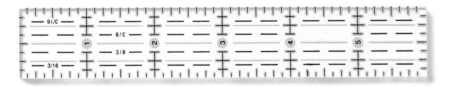

Fabric markers

Marking tools are used for transferring quilting patterns onto fabric, and for marking guidelines, so they need to make a strong line that can be removed without trace.

• Dressmaker's pens are fine felt-tips which give an ink line. They come in two types: one which fades completely in time and one which washes out.

• Quilter's pencils have a soft lead which can be sharpened to give a precise mark.

• Tailor's chalk makes a thicker, slightly waxy mark, which can be brushed away.

choosing fabrics

When you create your first piece of patchwork you will need a good variety of plain and patterned fabrics to work with, so start putting together a collection of scraps straight away. It is important however, to bear in mind is that only one type of fabric should be used in a quilt, ideally a hardwearing 100% cotton. Any synthetic content in the fibres should not exceed one third. Choose a firm square weave which is easy to stitch, especially along diagonal edges.

Finding new sources

You may already have a bulging rag-bag, full of remnants and offcuts left over from dressmaking, but be imaginative in your search for additional fabrics and scour market stalls and specialist ethnic importers for unusual materials. Don't be afraid to mix cultures and traditions: an African indigo resist or Indonesian batik will sit happily alongside a French Provençal floral print or fine Madras checks. If you are using new fabrics it is always a good idea to buy extra, if you are not sure how much you will need. It may not be possible to match a particular design and left-overs can always be incorporated in another project.

Prints and patterns

Once your search has begun there will be a seemingly endless variety of fabrics from which to select. Small-scale sprigs, all-over florals, spots, checks and ginghams are all long-standing favourites and blend together well. Stripes of all widths can be used to good visual effect by exploiting their geometric qualities. Some larger or vividly coloured prints may seem unpromising, but look at small areas within the overall pattern. A superficially unattractive fabric may yield interesting patches when it has been cut up. Lightweight furnishing fabrics such as flowered chintzes will introduce a different scale of pattern; look out also for quirky details – words or colour tests – printed along the selvedge, all of which add character to your work.

Recycling material

A quilt made entirely from new dressmaking and specially printed craft fabrics will look spectacular, but could prove expensive. Patchwork has always been a thrift craft and using cloth from discarded garments brings an element of personal history to a quilt. Old shirts, outgrown children's clothing, a favourite but out-of-date summer frock or the embroidered parts of an old tea cloth can all be given new life, but make sure you avoid any areas that may have worn thin. Dye plain fabrics such as sheeting in the washing machine and overdye existing prints to create your own colourways. The tiniest fragments of cloth can be used in your quilt, so swap pieces with your friends to build up a wide 'palette' with which to work. Some of the most fascinating quilts are made up of a random selection of fabrics.

Preparing the fabric

All new fabrics should be washed on a hot cycle to remove any surplus dye or dressing, and to prevent further shrinkage. This may take some time but it is well worth it in the long run, as you will not want the colours to bleed or the fabric to pucker if your finished quilt has to be laundered. Press all the fabric well, fold and store in clear plastic bags if you are not going to cut out the pieces straight away. The exception to this is glazed, chintz-like fabric which has a slightly shiny surface. If you want to preserve the smooth finish, make sure that it is used for an item that will only ever by dry-cleaned.

colour &
pattern

Your choice of fabrics will play just as important a part as the design itself in defining the look of your quilt. Be spontaneous when it comes to deciding which colours and patterns to put together and trust your own intuition. If you are making a quilt to go in a specific room you may want to match it to the existing furnishings, but otherwise, try not to have any preconceptions about which fabrics to use.

Contrasting shades

The key to colour is light: rich jewel-like shades absorb the sunlight in a brightly lit interior, while a darker room will be enlivened by clear, bright colours in paler shades. Light colours in a sunny room create an airy feeling of space. You can use colour to create an atmosphere, maybe based on your impression and memories of a favourite place – a flower-filled garden or the rosy glow of a Mediterranean sky.

Combining colours

If you are not sure how to start choosing your colours, try simply throwing an armful of fabrics across the floor. The accidental interplay of colours can produce random pairings and surprising combinations. Remember that colours do not always have to match, and the juxtaposition of opposite tones – coral and emerald or yellow and purple – will give an extra vibrancy.

Looking for inspiration

New and exciting visual sources are all around you. Study a favourite painting, postcard or scrap of printed fabric, to find colours that work well together. Pick out several in light, medium and dark shades, then match them up to plain and patterned materials from your collection. Cut a small sample of each, lay them out on the table and re-arrange the swatches to find a good balance of colour and texture. Add and take away pieces until you have a pleasing arrangement, then stick them down. Look at them again later, to see if you still like the selection you have made, and change it if necessary.

Mixing patterns and colour

Make sure that there is sufficient tonal contrast between your fabrics and plenty of variation in the pattern scale, or the impact of the patchwork will become lost, especially if it is to be quilted. You will find that the appearance of a fabric changes according to the other colours and patterns which surround it, so take time to experiment with different combinations. Put a dark but bright fabric together with a medium and a light shade to give life to the design. Too many small patterns in similar colourways will blend into a single overall texture, so always use a mix of bold and detailed prints, stripes, checks and plain colours.

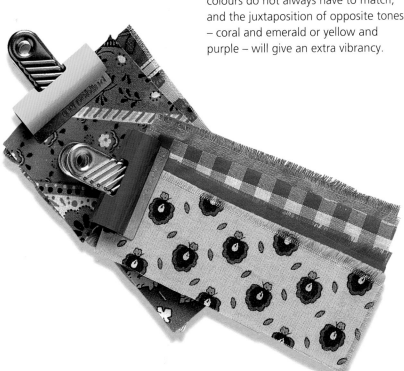

choosing your technique

You can stitch your patchwork by hand or machine, but the two techniques should not be thought of simply as alternative ways of achieving the same result. Each involves its own psychological approach and the method you choose will be a personal decision, depending not only on the amount of time and involvement you wish to dedicate, but also on the particular design you have chosen and the scale of the project. Both methods have their own special qualities, which you should consider carefully at the outset, but you may actually find yourself combining elements of hand and machine sewing to create the best result.

Machine patchwork

Sewing by machine has the great advantage of speed, especially when joining simple straight seams (fig 1), or adding borders and binding strips. Machine-piecing patchwork is the quickest way of making up any blocks which are based on squares, rectangles, and diagonal subdivisions such as right-angled triangles. The sharp, regular appearance of the seams complements all basic geometric patterns. Machine piecing should always be used for items which will have to withstand a lot of wear and tear or frequent laundering.

Hand patchwork

Hand-pieced patchwork is very different to machine piecing in scale, speed and appearance: the finished look is softer and the seams have a less harsh line. Although it takes longer to do, the technique enables you to create more involved patterns, using small shapes which would otherwise be difficult to join. Hexagons, diamonds and six-pointed stars should all be pieced this way (fig 2). The act of sewing by hand makes you more intimately involved with the fabric itself, and because you are not tied to the sewing machine, the work is portable.

Patchwork patterns

There is a great wealth of historic and traditional designs to draw on, which you can recreate or reinterpret in your own work. If you do not have a particular project in mind, spend some time researching the numerous sources which include design and needlework reference books, craft manuals, specialist magazines and museum collections. Study both old and new quilts to get an idea of the many exciting possibilities available.

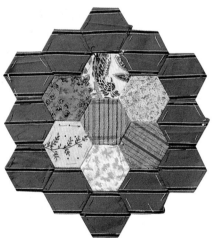

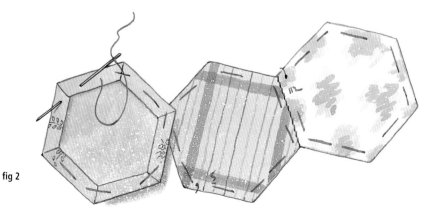

fig 1

fig 2

All-over patterns

Some of the most beautiful and complex quilts feature all-over designs, built up from one or more interlocking shapes. When a single shape is used the visual interest comes from the arrangement of colour within the repeat. The Stars & Diamonds Quilt (see page 92) and the Harlequin Quilt (see page 88) show how versatile this type of patchwork can be, when imaginatively used.

Block designs

Many nineteenth-century quilts are made from repeated pattern blocks, joined with plain squares or bands of fabric called sashing bars. The designs were figurative or geometric, and most were given evocative names to reflect the day-to-day lives of the women who stitched them – Flying Geese, Ships at Sea, Delectable Mountain and Bear's Paw. If you do not want to make a quilt in the traditional style, put several different blocks together to make a sample panel or a small throw.

New inspiration

Alternatively, you may prefer to create your own original design. Look at the diversity of patterns which surround you every day – tiled floors, wallpaper, furnishing fabrics, a woven rug or even the graphic design of packaging – for inspiration. Find a single motif, or an all-over pattern, that can be simplified or adapted for patchwork and give it a special name.

Adding a border

Many patchwork designs are complete in themselves but, like a well selected picture frame, a border can add greatly to others. It will emphasize but not detract from the centre panel. You may simply want to add plain bands of fabric with a subtle quilting, as on the Log Cabin Throw (see page 50) or adapt an element from the block so that the border becomes an integral part of the design. The Dresden Plate Quilt (see page 84) is a good example of this.

19

planning your design

As well as establishing the choice of pattern, fabrics and technique, you should consider carefully the size of the project you want to undertake, particularly if it is your first. A bedcover may take literally years to stitch and is a major commitment, so always make a sample block first. If it does not turn out how you expected, it can be adapted for another project at a later date – the flexibility and adaptability of patchwork is part of its appeal.

Defining a colour scheme

To get an idea of how your finished patchwork will look and to determine how to use your chosen fabrics, draw the pattern to scale on graph paper and make several photocopies. Try colouring in each sheet in a different way. By changing the fabric arrangement within the design you can emphasize different elements of the block, often producing startlingly different results. You will need to include a mixture of light, medium and dark shades to give life to the pattern. If you are making a small-scale piece, you could draw it up to size and fill in the shapes to represent fabrics you already have. This is a creative exercise in its own right, which will help you decide on the fabrics you want to use without having to cut up long-hoarded or precious remnants.

Working out fabric quantities

You will need to know the quantity required of each fabric you have chosen for your design, whether you are purchasing it specially or are using existing stocks. Using your scale drawing, count how many times each shape in each colour appears. Draw up actual-size templates. Measure the width and add on 2cm (¾in), then work out how many times it will fit into a standard fabric width of 114cm (45in). Calculate the length of fabric needed, based on the depth of the template plus 2cm (¾in).

When buying new material you should always get slightly more than you need, to allow for shrinkage or any mistakes in cutting out and calculations. Any left-overs can go straight into your fabric collection, ready to be used in the next project. If you are using random scraps for the motifs, you may only need to buy the background fabric, as for example in the Flying Geese quilt (see page 54). In this case you should buy the full amount at once, as you may not be able to match it later.

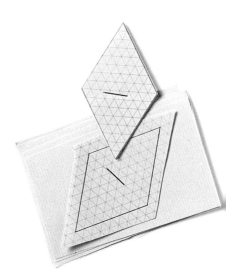

Starting off

Preparing the pieces

If you are embarking on a new project you will want to start sewing straight away, but the thought of cutting out hundreds of patches before you begin can seem a bit daunting. Depending on the amount of time you have available, it is easier to cut out in batches, or to prepare just enough shapes to use in a single sewing session. Plastic freezer bags with re-sealable edges are ideal for storing cut patchwork shapes. Label each one with the template reference letter or a name. Once the pieces have been cut out they should not be ironed, so do not let them get creased. When you are ready to sew the patches together, lay them all out flat on your work surface to get an idea of how the finished patchwork will look – this also gives you the opportunity to make any last minute changes. If, however, you are not happy with the pieces once they are assembled, do not hesitate to unpick them, and add in new colours. Always be flexible in your approach, and remember that any alterations are an integral part of the quilt's development.

Storing your work

If you are lucky enough to have a special sewing room or studio space, you can leave your patchwork out when you are not working on it. Cover it over with a sheet to keep off the dust. Sometimes you may not return to a piece for some months, so put it away in an old, clean pillowcase. Make sure that everything is labelled and well organized; it is easy to get pieces muddled up when you are not working with them. As you finish each block or section of the quilt, press it carefully. Stack the blocks up flat – they should not be folded – in a neat pile, and keep them in a drawer or cupboard until they are joined together.

Caring for your quilt

When your quilt is complete it can be laundered if you wish. You will find this adds extra texture to the surface by creating a slightly puckered effect in between the quilting stitches. If all the fabrics have been prepared properly, and you have used a polyester filling, it should not shrink. Set the machine to a gentle hand wash cycle, and spin gently but do not tumble dry. If possible, hang the quilt on a washing line and let it dry in the sun. Quilts that include non-colourfast fabrics may be dry-cleaned, but the chemicals used in the solvents can fade certain dyes.

The best way to display a full-size quilt is, of course, to spread it over your bed, but if your patchwork is not in daily use it should be wrapped up carefully in an old, clean sheet – never a plastic bag. Re-fold it from time to time, or the creases will become permanent. A finished piece of quilting should never be pressed or it will loose its characteristic 'body'. If you have enough space, keep it rolled up in a long bolster shape.

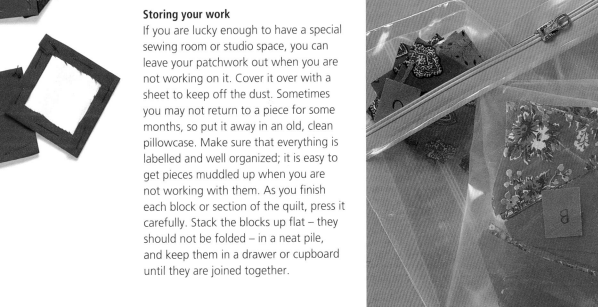

Squares, stars & stripes

The first prototype sewing machine was patented in 1846 by the American Elias Howe, and as his invention became affordable and more widely available in subsequent years, it was seized on by seamstresses and quilt makers as a liberating, labour-saving device.

Even if you are not an experienced dressmaker, you will find that it still does not take long to piece patchwork by machine. The speed with which a beginner can produce exciting and interesting designs, experiment with colour and pattern, and turn ideas into reality should inspire you to explore this fascinating and creative needlecraft.

how to piece by machine

Machine piecing does not involve any complicated skills and you will only need a basic straight stitch to sew your patches together. The accuracy of the finished work depends mainly on precise cutting out of both templates and fabric. If you are not used to machine stitching on a smaller scale, it is worth practising narrow seams on scrap material before you start on a special project. Set the stitch length to approximately 20 per 5cm (10 per 1in) and adjust the tension to give a regular, even seam. Stitch slowly, guiding the pieces with both hands. Always use a sharp, medium-gauge needle and a thread type to suit the fabric weight.

Making the templates

The templates for all the projects are given at the back of the book. Trace those which are shown at full size or photocopy the ones which need to be enlarged. Draw any other shapes up on graph paper using a ruler and sharp pencil as indicated. Add the grain lines and reference letter so that they can be identified easily. A seam allowance of 6mm (¼in) is included within each patch; the stitching line is shown as a guide only and does not have to be transferred. Cut out each one roughly, stick onto to thin card and, using a craft knife, cutting mat and metal ruler, cut around the outlines.

Following the grain

The templates are marked with a line which indicates the direction in which the grain, or weave, of the fabric must lie. Always follow this or the patches, especially squares and rectangles, will become distorted. Some shapes, such as triangles and diamonds, have diagonal sides, which have to be cut on the bias. To prevent the points pulling, ensure that the adjacent side always runs along the grain.

Marking out the patches

The pieces should be cut out so that they make the most of any printed or woven design on the fabric, so it is worth taking time to plan your layout before marking the shapes. Line up stripes and checks so that they will form their own patterns within the patchwork and centre small motifs where appropriate (this may mean ignoring the grain). Draw carefully around the template onto the right side of the cloth with a sharp-tipped fabric marker and cut out (fig 1). Use a light line on dark fabrics and a dark line to show up on light fabrics. Try to fit the shapes together as closely as you can to avoid wasting any fabric.

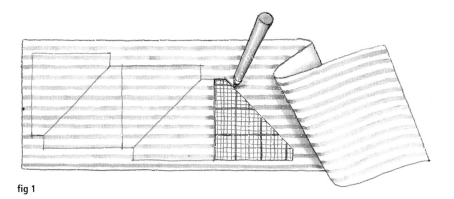

fig 1

fig 2

Using a rotary cutter

Bulk cutting your patches with a rotary cutter and quilter's ruler will save a lot of time. Take four pieces of fabric the same size, stack them the same way up and press. Mark the templates onto the top piece, then cut out each shape through all the layers. Keep the handle upright so that the blade runs along the side of the ruler's edge and always push away from you (fig 2). The parallel lines marked on the ruler will enable you to cut precise squares, rectangles and strips if you line them up to the straight edge of the fabric to give the width you require.

Joining straight edges

Place the two pieces to be joined together, with right sides facing. Match the corners exactly and pin the edge at right angles. When joining the short sides of right-angled triangles, sew from the corner to the point to prevent the narrow end getting caught in the feed dog (fig 3). The templates include a seam allowance of 6mm (¼in). Depending on your machine, this is usually the distance between the needle and the right side of the presser foot: if not, you can stick a piece of masking tape on the machine bed, at the correct distance. Keeping the outside edges of the fabric lined up to the mark or the foot, sew the pieces together. The foot should pass over the pins. Instead of snipping the thread between patches, you can speed up your sewing by chain piecing. Leaving a short length of thread between each pair, pass them under the foot one after another, to make what looks like a row of bunting (fig 4). Cut the threads to separate them.

Joining diagonals

Fabric can stretch when it has been cut on the bias, so try to avoid handling the long edges of triangles and the sides of diamonds, and do not press them once they have been cut out. Match the points and corners together and pin at right angles to the seam (fig 5).

Pressing the seams

Clip off any long ends of thread and press the seam allowances to one side, using a hot iron without any steam. Use a pressing rather than a gliding action to avoid distorting the stitch line. When a dark and light patch have been joined together, you should press the allowance under the darker fabric to avoid it showing through.

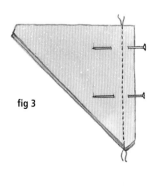

fig 3

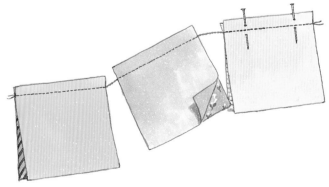

fig 4

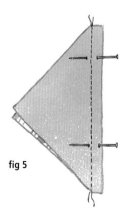

fig 5

Matching seams

When you have three seams meeting up, make sure that the allowances are pressed in opposite directions to avoid bulky joins. With right sides facing, match the seam lines exactly and pin before stitching together (fig 6).

Squaring up

When a number of separate pieces have been machine stitched together to make a block, a small degree of distortion is inevitable. Always make sure that the edges are accurate when the patchwork is finished. If they are not, you will need to redraw the outline with a set square and fabric marker. Trim to realign the edges into a perfect square or rectangle before joining the blocks (fig 7).

fig 6

Instant patchwork

Machine piecing and rotary cutting enable you to take many shortcuts. These two methods of making square and diamond patchworks are effective and quick to do. For a square pattern, cut several strips of fabric, all the same

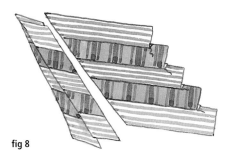

fig 8

length and roughly the same width. Join them together widthways and press the seam allowances in the same direction. Using the cutter and a quilter's ruler cut a series of multicoloured strips. Sew them back together, reversing the direction of alternate strips.

To make diamonds, join the strips together so that the ends are stepped, then cut across them at a 45 degree angle (fig 8). Sew the strips together, reversing the direction of some, then square off the edges (fig 9).

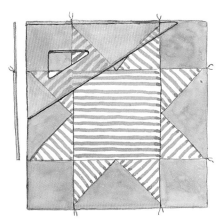

fig 7

fig 9

mosaic cushions

Making these multi-coloured cushion covers will give you the perfect excuse to sort out your rag-bag and put those hoarded remnants of fabric to good use. Even the tiniest postage-stamp size scraps can be included, to produce colourful designs which involve only the most basic straight seaming. Depending on the size of your fabric pieces, the stripes and squares can be sewn together individually or, for a speedier result, with the seam and cut method on page 26. This technique will produce a less random appearance, but you could use a mixture of both techniques to use up all your material.

Square cushion

You will need

for a cover 44 x 42cm (17¾ x 16½in):
Assorted scraps in various prints
25 x 45cm (10 x 18in) light brown print
75 x 80cm (30 x 32in) blue chambray
Matching sewing thread
2 buttons
40cm (16in) square cushion pad

To cut out

10 4 x 32cm (1½ x 13in) strips of
  different fabric or 110 4 x 5cm (1½ x
  2in) rectangles in assorted prints
2 5 x 32cm (2 x 12½in) & 2 5 x 41cm
  (2 x 16½in) strips in light brown
4 7 x 75cm (3 x 30in) strips & 2 25 x 42
  (10 x 17in) rectangles in blue
  chambray

To make the patchwork

1 If you are working with small patches, join them into ten rows, each of eleven rectangles. Seam across the long edges, leaving a 6mm (¼in) allowance. The pieces can be joined haphazardly, but if you want to ensure a good balance of colour and pattern, arrange them before joining. Press the seams to one side, then join together lengthways and press.

2 Alternatively, join the ten strips together with 6mm (¼in) seams. Press the allowance to one side, then cut into 10 4cm (1½in) strips using a rotary cutter or scissors. Rejoin the strips to make a rectangle, reversing the direction of every other one (see page 27).

3 Square off the patchwork to 32 x 34cm (13in x 14in). Sew the 32cm (13in) light brown strips to the short edges and press the seams outwards. Join the other two light brown strips to the long edges and press.

To make the frill

4 Join the four chambray strips into a loop and press in half widthways with wrong sides facing. Matching the raw edges and pin the loop to the cushion front so that the seams line up with the corners. Working from the corners inwards, fold and pin six 1.5cm (⅝in) pleats at either side of each corner (fig 1). Tack the frill securely in place.

To finish off

5 Press under 6mm (¼in), then 3cm (1¼in) along one long edge of each back panel. Tack, then top stitch the turnings in place to make a facing. Work two buttonholes, each 14cm (5½in) in from the edge, on one panel.

6 With right sides facing, place the panel with the buttonholes to the left edge of the cushion front and the other panel to the right edge. Pin, then stitch together around all four sides, 1cm (⅜in) from the edge (fig 2). Clip the corners and turn right side out, then top stitch right around the edge of the cover. Sew the buttons to the lower panel, in line with the buttonholes.

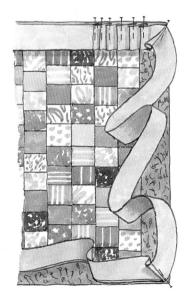

fig 1

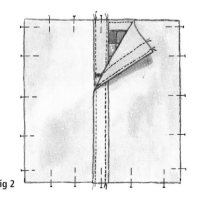

fig 2

Striped cover

You will need

for a cover 45 x 35cm (18 x 14in)
Assorted scraps, each at least 11cm (4½in) long
8 x 26cm (3 x 10in) blue floral
40 x 85cm (16 x 34in) calico
38 x 50cm (15 x 20in) cushion pad

To cut out

for the front
2 4 x 26cm (1½ x 10in) strips in blue floral
57 2–3 x 10cm (¾–1¼ x 4in) strips
2 6 x 35.5cm (2½in x 14in) & 2 14 x 38cm (5½ x 15in) strips in calico
for the back, facings & ties
2 9 x 38cm (3½ x 15in) strips & 1 38 x 50cm (15 x 20in) rectangle in calico
8 4 x 20cm (1½ x 8in) strips, 2 each in 4 colours

To make the cushion front

1 Piece together three rows of nineteen coloured strips, leaving seam allowances of 6mm (¼in). Sew together by stitching the blue floral bands between them (fig 3), then join one of the narrow calico strips to each long side. Press the seam towards the calico.

2 Press under 6mm (¼in) along one long edge of each of the other two strips,

then press in half widthways. With right sides facing, pin and stitch the raw edges to the short sides. Turn back along the fold so that the neatened edge covers the edge of the patchwork. Pin in place, then top stitch from the front, 3mm (⅛in) from the edge of the calico (fig 4).

To finish off

3 Stitch a narrow single hem along one long edge of the two facing strips, then sew one to each short side of the back. Fold the front and back pieces in half widthways and mark the centre of the top and bottom edges with pins. Place the two pieces with right sides together, lining up these points (fig 5). Fold the facings over the cushion front and pin along both sides, then stitch 1cm (⅜in) from the edge. Neaten the seam allowance with a zigzag and turn right side out.

4 Make the ties by pressing under 1cm (⅜in) along each edge of the strips, then pressing them in half widthways. Tack together, then top stitch around all four sides, close to the outside edge (fig 6). Matching the pairs, slip stitch to the inside of the cover, 10cm (4in) in from the corners. Insert the cushion pad and do up the ties.

fig 3

fig 4

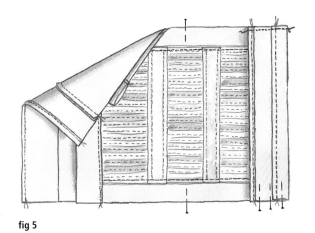

fig 5

fig 6

toys & trifles

These three-dimensional cut outs are a good way to utilise your first experimental pieces of machine patchwork. They can be filled with lavender and flower petals to make scented pillows, or with toy stuffing to create an idiosyncratic gift for a favourite small boy or girl.

Lace-up shoe and Victorian boot

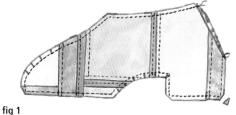

fig 1

You will need

for the shoe
30cm (12in) square of patchwork
60cm (24in) narrow silk cord
Large eyed needle
for the boot
30 x 35cm (12 x 14in) patchwork
3mm (⅛in) ruby glass beads
15cm (6in) narrow fabric tape or
   15cm(6in) decorative braid
Fine needle
for both
Polyester toy filling or dried herbs &
   flowers
Matching sewing cotton

To cut out

Photocopy the boot or shoe templates on page 98 to 200%. Cut two pieces from the patchwork. Remember to reverse the template for the second piece.

To make up

1 Pin the two shapes together with right sides facing. Machine stitch along the seam line, leaving a space between *a* and *a*. Clip the corners and notch the curves (fig 1), then turn right sides out. Use a knitting needle to ease out the angles, then stuff with wadding. Close the gap with slip stitch.

To finish the shoe

2 Thread a large-eyed needle with the silk cord and stitch through the front of the shoe at the points marked. Tie the ends into a bow.

To finish the boot

3 Start off the fringed edging by fastening a double length of thread 1cm (⅜in) from one end of the tape. Thread on approximately 40 beads, bring the needle through the back of the tape to form a loop and secure with a small double stitch. Repeat at 6mm (¼in) intervals along the tape (fig 2), then stitch the tape around the top of the boot. (You should omit the fringe if the boot is for a very young child). Alternatively sew on your own purchased trimming around the edge.

fig 2

Scottie dog

This toy is inspired by a motif that appears on an American quilt made by Alice Brooks in the 1930s. She had based it on a much-loved dog which belonged to President Roosevelt – a good example of how quilt makers from one generation can influence the work of their successors.

You will need

18 x 24cm (7 x 9½in) patchwork
30cm (12in) square of light blue cotton
Polyester filling or dried herbs & flowers
Matching sewing cotton
Red sewing cotton

To cut out

Photocopy the templates on page 97 to 200%. Cut two of each shape, reversing the second pieces.
2 C & 2 D in light blue
2 B in patchwork

To make up

1 On a 15 x 26cm (6 x 10in) rectangle of blue cotton mark a 3cm (1¼in) grid, parallel to the sides, and stitch over the lines with red thread. Press, then cut out the two A pieces.

2 Sort out the pieces for each side of the dog, and make up both in the same way. Sew the head A to body B, matching points *a* and *b*. Join the back leg C to the body at *c* and *d* and the front leg at *e* and *f* (fig 3). Press the seams outwards, then top stitch with red thread.

3 Pin the pieces together and stitch along the seam line, leaving a space between *g* and *g*. Clip the corners, notch the curves and turn through. Use a knitting needle to ease out the ears, paws and tail, then fill with wadding. Close the gap with slip stitch.

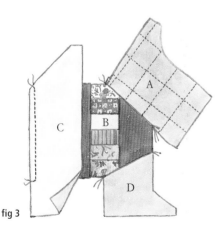

fig 3

33

simply stars

The simple eight-pointed star and strong colours of these cushions reflect the patchwork designs created by the Amish and Shaker communities in the nineteenth century, but they have a essentially timeless appeal and modernity. The tie-on covers are recycled from plain and dyed cotton sheeting, which has been matched with a crisp blue-and-white gingham.

Blue-and-white cushion

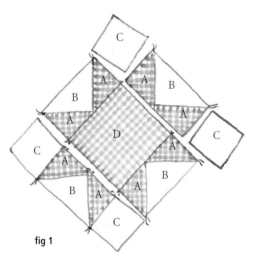

fig 1

You will need

for a cover 60cm (24in) square
50 x 60cm (20 x 24in) gingham
150 x 114cm (60 x 45in) white
10cm (4in) square of red
Matching sewing cotton
60cm (24in) cushion pad

To cut out

for the patchwork
32 A & 4 D in gingham
16 B, 16 C, 4 E, 4 F & 1 16cm (6¼in)
    square H in white
for the border
4 D in white
4 G in red
8 3 x 9cm (1¼ x 3½in) & 4 3 x 45cm
    (1¼ x 18in) strips in gingham
for the back & ties
20 x 61cm (8 x 24½in) rectangle &
    61cm (24½in) square in white
4 7 x 25 (3 x 10in) strips in gingham

To make the cushion front

1 Sew the diagonal sides of two A triangles to either side of a B triangle to make a rectangle. Make four of these, then press the seams outwards. Join a C square to the short sides of two of the rectangles and press the seams inwards. Sew the other two rectangles to either side of a D square so that the A triangles point outwards. Add the two strips to the top and bottom (fig 1) and press the seams towards the centre. Make four star blocks in this way.

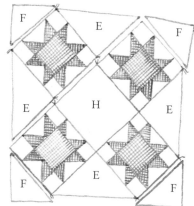

fig 2

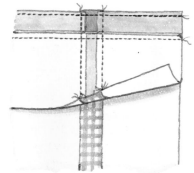

fig 3

2 Join a triangle E to either side of two star blocks. Sew the other star blocks to either side of the large square H and join the three rows together. Sew a triangle F to each corner (fig 2).

3 Sew the long gingham border strips to the white strips, leaving a 6mm (¼in) seam allowance, then join two strips M to opposite sides of the patchwork. Press the seams towards the gingham.

4 Stitch a short gingham strip along one side of a square D, and join another to the end of a red square G. Sew the two pieces together, matching the seams. Make four of these blocks, then sew one to either end of the two long border strips (fig 3). Join to the other two sides of the patchwork and then press the seams towards the gingham.

fig 4

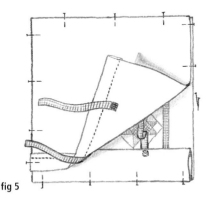
fig 5

Red-and-blue cushion

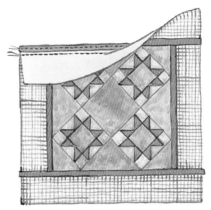
fig 6

To finish off

5 Make the ties by pressing under 1cm (⅜in) along each edge of the gingham strips, then pressing them in half widthways. Tack together, then top stitch around all four sides, close to the outside edge (fig 4).

6 Press the white strip in half widthways to make the facing. Stitch two ties to the folded edge, 20cm (8in) in from the sides. With right sides facing and the ties underneath, pin along one side of the cushion front, matching the raw edges.

7 Press under 1cm (⅜in), then 5cm (2in) along one edge of the white back square to make a deep hem, then stitch in place. Mark two points on the right side, 8cm (3in) in from the hemmed edge and 20cm (8in) in from the sides. Sew the other two ties to these points.

8 With right sides facing, place the back over the cushion front so that the folded edge lies across the centre of the facing and the raw edges line up (fig 5). Pin in place, then stitch all around the four sides, 1cm (⅜in) from the edge. Clip the corners and neaten the allowance with a zigzag. Turn through, insert the pad and fasten the ties.

You will need

for a cover 64cm (25in) square
120 x 114cm (48 x 24in) gingham
70 x 80cm (28 x 32in) blue
30 x 65cm (12 x 26in) red
Matching sewing cotton
64cm (25in) cushion pad

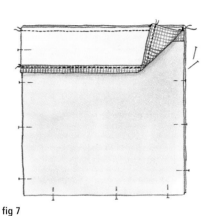
fig 7

To cut out

for the patchwork
32 A in red
16 B, 16 C, 4 D, 4 E, 4 F & 1 16cm (6¼in) square H in blue
for the border
2 4 x 45cm (1½ x 18in) & 2 4 x 66cm (1½ x 26½in) strips in red
2 9 x 45cm (3½ x 18in) & 2 9 x 66cm (3½ x 26½in) strips in gingham
for the back & ties
1 66 x 70cm (26½ x 28in) rectangle, 1 18 x 66cm (7 x 26½in) facing strip & 4 9 x 25 (3½ x 10in) tie strips in gingham

To make the cushion front

1 Make up the patchwork centre as for the Blue-and-white cushion.

2 Sew the short red strips to the short gingham strips, and the long red strips to the long gingham strips. Join the short pieces to opposite sides of the square and press the seams towards the red strips. Sew the long strips to the other two sides and press (fig 6).

To finish off

3 Press under 1cm (⅜in), then 3cm (1¼in) to make a hem at one short end of the back piece and stitch down close to the first fold. Make a narrow double hem along one long edge of the facing strip. With right sides together, pin and stitch the raw edge to one long border strip on the cushion front.

4 Pin the three raw edges of the front and back together with right sides facing. Fold the facing over the back piece and pin the short sides (fig 7). Stitch the three sides together, 1cm (⅜in) from the edge, then clip the corners and zigzag the seam allowance. Turn right side out.

5 Make the ties as in step 5 for the Blue-and-white cushion, then slip stitch two to the front and two to the back of the facing, 15cm (6in) in from the side, so that the stitches do not show through. Press, then top stitch the opening, 3mm (⅛in) from the edge.

ohio star throw

This square throw illustrates just how versatile one simple motif can be – it features the same eight-pointed star as the cushions on page 34, but this time each block has been made from two different fabrics. The key to producing a lively and interesting surface is to select scraps of various different patterns – paisleys, stripes, large- and small-scale florals – which all lie within a similar range of colours. The autumnal tones of rusts, browns and golden yellows used here give a rich warmth to the finished piece.

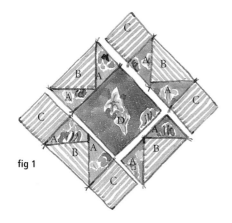

fig 1

You will need

for a throw 81cm (32in) square
Scraps of 34 different fabrics including florals, checks and stripes
15 x 70cm (6 x 28in) dark green
50 x 80cm (20 x 32in) red floral
83cm (33in) square of backing fabric
Matching sewing thread

To cut out

for each of the nine stars
8 A & 1 D in colour 1
4 B & 4 C in colour 2
8 E, 4 F & 4 15.2cm (6in) squares G in different fabrics
for the border
2 3.5 x 70cm (1⅜ x 28in) & 2 3.5 x 66cm (1⅜ x 26in) strips in dark green
2 11.5 x 70cm (4½in 28in) & 2 11.5 x 89 (4½ x 35in) strips in red floral

To make the star blocks

1 Join a triangle A to each side of the triangles B to make four rectangles. Press seams outwards. Add a square C to each short end of two rectangles and press seams inwards. Sew the other two rectangles to both sides of square D, press seams outwards. Sew the three strips together to form a square (fig 1), matching the seams carefully and press seams inwards. Make each star in a different combination of colours.

To make the quilt top

2 Lay out the blocks in three rows of three, then add the squares and triangles using fig 2 as a guide. Re-arrange them until you have a pleasing balance of colour and pattern. Sew the blocks, squares G and triangles E & F together in five diagonal rows. Pin the first two rows so that the seams line up, and stitch together. Press the seams to one side, then add the remaining rows in the same way. Complete the quilt top by sewing the triangles D to the corners.

3 Make the border by sewing a short green strip to either side of the quilt top and trimming the ends. Sew the two long strips to the remaining sides and square off. Press the seams outwards. Sew on the short and then the long red strips in the same way, and press the seams inwards (fig 3).

To finish off

4 Press under 4cm (1½in) along each edge of the quilt top, and mitre the corners. Trim the backing fabric to the same size as the top, then press under 2cm (¾in) all round. Pin the two layers together with wrong sides facing so that there is an equal margin all round, then slip stitch the backing in place (fig 4).

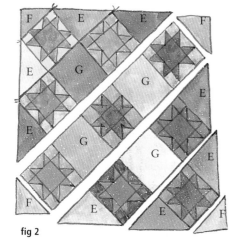

fig 2

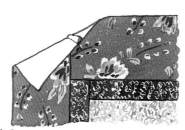

fig 3

fig 4

Quilting

The process of quilting brings life to your patchwork and gives it a new tactile quality. The stitches add further decoration to the design and, by increasing the play of light and shade across the surface of the fabric, change the pieced fabric into a three-dimensional textile.

Hand quilting does not produce instant results, but the hours you invest will add immeasurably to the finished piece. It may take many weeks to complete a bedcover – but take time to get into the rhythm of stitching and evolve your own personal way of working. You'll find that, with practice, quilting becomes a contemplative and relaxing pastime, enjoyable for its own sake.

preparing for quilting

A quilt consists of three layers: the decorative top, a plain backing and sandwiched between them the wadding, which gives it body and warmth. Quilting is the name given both to the process of stitching these layers together and to the stitches themselves. Once you have finished sewing your patchwork, the temptation is to start quilting straight away, but it is important to spend time at this stage planning and preparing the quilt itself, and making sure that it is properly tacked.

Choosing the wadding

Wadding gives the quilt its thickness and weight, and the finished appearance will depend on the type of filling. Take into account how much quilting you will do, the purpose of the quilt and how often it will need to be laundered.

fig 1

• Woollen blankets, that have been well worn and washed over the years, can be recycled as quilt fillings. This method of padding produces quite a heavy quilt, which does not require dense stitching. The quilt can be machine washed on a cool setting, but not spin-dried.
• Domette is a soft woven cotton fabric used for curtain interlining, which comes in light and medium weights. It will give a flat look to the finished bedcover, similar to antique examples, and it tends to shrink when washed. To prevent any distortion, the lines of quilting should not be more than 4cm (1½in) apart.
• Polyester batting is available in weights from 60g to 220g, which vary in thickness from 5mm (¼in) to 15mm (⅜in). It can be bought by length, or in pre-packaged squares big enough for a large bedcover. Polyester-filled quilts will be lighter and puffier than ones with a woven lining and as it does not shrink or shift when washed, the quilting stitches can be further apart. Thin polyester is best for machine quilting, as it is easy to manoeuvre under the presser foot. It is essential to use the lightest weight flameproof batting for a small child's cot or bedcover.

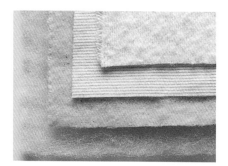

Cutting out the wadding
The wadding should be at least 10cm (4in) larger all round than the top, to allow for the inevitable changes of shape and size that occur during quilting. If you are making a large bedcover you may need to join two lengths to make the filling the correct size. An overlapped seam creates a bulky ridge, so the pieces should be butted together and joined with a loose herringbone stitch (fig 1).

Cutting out the backing
The backing can match or complement the quilt top, and should be of a similar weight. You may want to pick out a colour or pattern featured in the patchwork but, as a double bedcover will take up to 5m (5½yd) of fabric, a cheaper fabric can be used. Machine wash it on a hot cycle to pre-shrink and remove any dressing, then press and remove the selvedges. Sew the pieces together as necessary with a 1cm (⅜in) seam, and press the seams open. Like the wadding, the backing should be at least 10cm (4in) larger all round than the top – it is always easier to trim back than to sew on extra fabric.

Assembling the quilt

Whether you are making a small crib cover or a large bedspread, the three layers must be secured firmly together with safety pins and/or rows of tacking across the entire surface. You will be working on the quilt over a period of time, and it will need to be folded and put away when you are not working on it. Insufficient tacking will mean that the layers will shift during storage and quilting, causing an uneven, puckered surface. Depending on the size of your piece you can work on the floor, a stripped-down bed or a table top, but be sure to vacuum clean or dust the surface before you start.

Basting

Basting a large quilt

1 Always tack a large quilt together in two stages to ensure that the layers do not become creased. Lay the wadding out flat and place the backing centrally over it, right side up. Smooth the two layers with the flat of your hand.

2 Using a big needle and dark thread,  sew four lines of long (about 4cm/1½in) tacking stitches from the centre to the mid-point of each side. Continuing to work from the centre out, stitch a grid across each quarter section in turn (fig 2). The lines should be between 8cm (3in) to 10cm (4in) apart, but do not worry if they are uneven. Start each with a knot and finish with a loose backstitch. Do not pull the thread too tightly. Turn the quilt over.

3 Press the patchwork to remove any creases. This is the last time it will be ironed, as a finished quilt should never be pressed or it will lose its texture. Place the top centrally on the wadding, with the right side up, so that there is an equal margin all round. Smoothing as you stitch, tack in place as before (fig 3).

Basting a small quilt

All three layers of a cot quilt can be joined together at the same time. When working on a smaller scale you may find it quicker to use a combination of tacking and safety pins: either special quilter's pins or standard 5cm (2in) pins. Place the patchwork and wadding centrally onto the backing and smooth out. Pin from the centre outwards at 15cm (6in) intervals across the quilt top (fig 4), then pin around the edge.

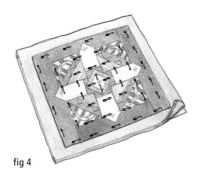

fig 2

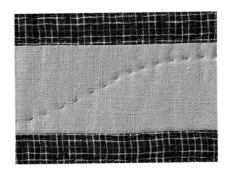

fig 3

fig 4

How to quilt

Quilting serves two purposes: as well as holding the layers together, it brings an element of texture to the pieced surface of the patchwork. The actual sewing involves nothing more complicated than a running stitch, but the more stitching you do, the more pattern and depth the finished piece will have.

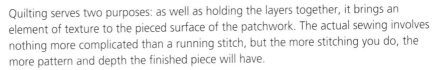

• If you have basted your quilt sufficiently you may find quilting hoops and frames are not necessary. A large hoop, around 40cm (15in) in diameter, will, however, isolate just one area of the quilt and keep it taut. Always take the quilt out of the ring when it is not in use, so that it does not become marked.

• Quilting is usually worked with white thread, but if you use a matching colour the stitches will become less visible and the pattern will be thrown into relief. If you want the stitches to become a feature in themselves, use a contrasting thread and make them bolder.

• The thread should not be any longer than 40cm (16in) to prevent it from becoming tangled. Don't stitch right to the end of the length if it has started to fray, or the stitches may snap.

• Always begin stitching from the centre and progress out towards the edges so that the surface does not become puckered. If your quilt is made up of repeated blocks, outline quilt each block first, then work the detail afterwards.

• Avoid stitching through tacking threads, as this will make them difficult to unpick.

Quilting stitch

This is a variation on basic running stitch, which is worked through all three layers of the quilt. The stitches should be regular and the same length both front and back, but their size depends on the effect you want. Thicker wadding means that you will have to make large stitches – up to five per 2.5cm (1in) – but the finest work may require up to twice that number. Do not pull the thread too tightly.

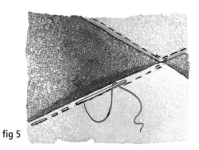

fig 5

Starting and finishing off

There should be no knots on a quilt, as they can work loose. Begin each row of stitching by inserting the needle about 5cm (2in) away from where you want to begin. Bring it up at the start point and carefully pull the thread through until the end disappears in the wadding, then work three small backstitches over each other to secure (fig 5). Finish off each row in the same way, by working a small treble stitch. Pass the end of the thread through the quilt, pull to the surface and clip so that the tail stays below the fabric.

Working the quilting

Sit with the hand that you sew with on top of the quilt and the other below.

You must always wear a thimble on your sewing finger to push the needle through the thick layers, and protect the other hand with a second thimble or quilter's shield on the first finger. If you are making a bedcover, roll up the areas that are not being worked on and fix them with safety pins. Rest the quilt on a table, or the arms of a chair if possible, to prevent its weight pulling on the stitches. All this may seem awkward to start with, but you will soon find the way of working that suits you best. Concentrate at first on making sure that the stitches are all the same size and evenly spaced. Once you have done that, you can try making them smaller if you wish.

Quilting patterns

When planning your quilting design, decide whether you want to make a special feature of the stitching or to use it just to highlight the patchwork. Complex shapes need only minimal outlining, but borders, sashing and background areas can be filled in with new patterns. Fine and detailed quilting shows up best on white or single-coloured material but tends to get lost on all-over printed fabrics. Some bedcovers, such as the old Welsh and Durham wholecloth quilts, are made up entirely of intricate quilting patterns on a plain fabric. The White Quilt on page 58 is made up with an embroidered linen tablecloth as its centre, and continues this tradition.

Outline quilting

This method of quilting is used to accentuate the lines within a patchwork design. It can be worked in three ways, each with a different effect.
• Work the stitching 3–6mm (⅛–¼in) from the seam, either inside or outside the edge of the shape (fig 6). This will give a slightly raised look to the pieces.

• Stitch along the seam itself if you do not want the quilting to be obvious. Known as sewing 'in the ditch', this technique is also used to disguise the harder line of machine quilting (fig 7).
• Add interest to a large area of printed fabric by outlining the shapes within it – flower motifs, stripes or gingham checks (fig 8).

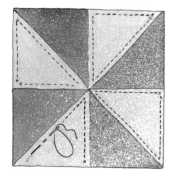

fig 6

fig 7

fig 8

Free quilting

The stitched line can be used to 'draw' new patterns in plain areas. There are many beautiful old quilting patterns, including wreaths, waves, feathers, scallops and garlands, but straight lines can be equally effective.

• Give extra emphasis by stitching with a double line. Parallel lines and trellis patterns are easy to draw if you use a quilter's ruler as a guide (fig 9).
• Individual motifs can be designed to echo the patchwork patterns within the quilt (fig 10).

fig 9

fig 10

Marking the design

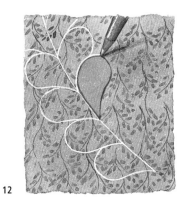

fig 11

Although it is possible to mark up the whole surface of a quilt before you start stitching, you may find it easier to draw the outlines as you go, working on one area at a time. This is, of course, the only way to work if you are using a fading pen, but other types of marker may rub off before you have finished stitching.

Outline quilting can be done by eye, following the patchwork shapes. However, if you feel that you need a guideline to start with, try sticking low-tack 6mm (¼in) wide masking tape along the seam and stitching along the edge of it. Peel the tape off straight away, to avoid marking the fabric.
• Parallel lines and trellis patterns can be marked directly onto the cloth with a quilter's ruler and a fading pen or chalk marker. The ruler is made of clear plastic marked with a right-angled grid, so the lines can be drawn at any distance apart.
• Free quilting, despite its name, needs to follow well defined lines. Cut a template from thin card: either one of your own

design, or following the outline given for the project you are making. If the motif has a pattern within it, such as the veins on a leaf or the lines that divide the points of a star, trace these onto the card and cut along them, stopping just short of the end (fig 11). Place the template onto the quilt and draw around the edge, then fill in any internal lines. Patterns which consist of one repeated element are built up from a single template. Rule a centre line for a symmetrical design, then draw the required number of outlines along either side, reversing the template for the second side (fig 12). For a round garland or swag, two templates are given – for the inside and outside of the curve.

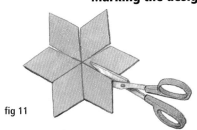

fig 12

Machine quilting

This is much faster than hand quilting and gives a harder, more defined line. The finished effect is not as decorative, but it is functional and good for smaller pieces that will receive hard wear. All the layers of the quilt should be closely tacked or pinned together to prevent them shifting under the foot. If you are going to do a lot of machine quilting, get a 'walking foot' which reduces movement of the layers.

• Set the stitch to approximately 8 or 9 stitches per 2.5cm (1in) and the tension so that it is slightly looser than normal to prevent the wadding looking pinched. Sew slowly and carefully between the pieces. To turn a corner, raise the foot with the needle down, pivot the work round, then lower the foot and continue. An open 'quilting foot' makes it easier to follow the needle's path.

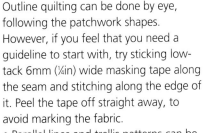

sampler rug

This rug is a true thrift quilt, which utilizes the tiniest scraps of cloth. Its appeal comes from a spontaneous combination of colour and pattern, and it should be approached in an informal way. You can follow the steps given below, or adapt the design to incorporate any practice pieces of machined squares, diamonds or stripes you have already made. These random blocks are mixed with naive pictorial motifs: a flower basket, a house, a boat and two stars. If you don't want to embark on a large project, try sewing a single block and make it up into a cushion cover. The rug is machine quilted with a polyester wadding, so it will stand up to laundering and daily wear and tear. Follow the placement diagram on page 48.

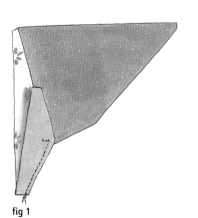

You will need

for a rug 110 x 125cm (44 x 49in)
Scraps and remnants of assorted fabrics, totalling at least 150cm (60in) square. The pieces should include some long strips to frame the blocks and for the ends of the rug. Precise quantities for the motif blocks are given below
50 x 128cm (20 x 50in) blue cotton
110 x 120cm (44 x 48in) backing fabric
110 x 120cm (44 x 48in) polyester wadding
Matching sewing thread
Navy sewing thread for quilting

To cut out all over

All-over blocks (2, 4, 5 & 6) and frames 3–6cm (1¼–2½in) wide strips in various lengths and fabrics
The templates for the other blocks are at the back of the book
for the border strips
6 5 x 97cm (2 x 39in) in different prints
2 12 x 97cm (5 x 39in) & 2 12 x 130cm (5 x 52in) in blue

To work the Faceted stars

Choose contrasting dark, light and mid-tone fabrics to make this elegant star look really three-dimensional. The two blocks are made up in different colourways. The colours used here are for the second star.

You will need

15 x 30cm (6 x 12in) white
15 x 30cm (6 x 12in) dark red
24 x 30cm (10 x 12in) mid blue

To cut out

4 A & 4 F in white
4 C & 4 D in dark red
4 B & 4 E in mid blue

To make the blocks

1 The star is made from four identical squares, each consisting of two mirror-image triangles. For the first one, sew a white point A to the left side of background piece B. Press the seam towards B. Pin a dark red point C to the lower edge of A. Stitch to 6mm (¼in) from the edge (fig 1), then pivot C so that the next side lies along the bottom of B. Pin, then stitch together. Clip the seam allowance and press.
2 Assemble the second triangle in the same way, by sewing a white F and a dark red D to background piece E. Stitch the two diagonally to form a square. Make three more squares, then join in pairs to form two rectangles (fig 2). Stitch these together to complete the block, sewing carefully over the thick layers of fabric in the centre.

fig 1

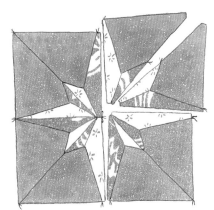

fig 2

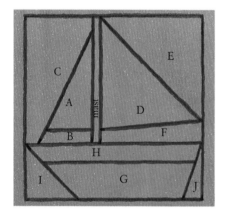

To work the Diamond block

3 Put together seven 23 x 3.5cm (9 x 1½in) diamond strips (see technique on page 26). Join them lengthwise, alternating the direction of the strips as you sew to create a chevron effect.

To work the Sailing boat block

The red check sails of this jaunty boat are cut from two separate triangles and the seam between them is concealed by the appliquéd mast.

To cut out

1 A & 1 D in red check
1 B, 1 C,1 E, 1 F, 1 I & 1 J in dark blue
1 G in striped print
1 H & 1 mast in mid blue

To make up the Sailing boat block

4 Sew sail A to B, then sew C along the diagonal edge. Join E, then F to sail D. Sew the two rectangles together and press the centre seam open. Press under 6mm (¼in) along each long edge of the mast and tack it over the seam (fig 3). Top stitch in place, 3mm (⅛in) from each side.
5 Join H to the top of G to make the boat, then stitch I and J to the two ends, making a rectangle. Sew the top edge of the boat to the sails.

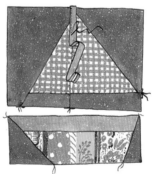

fig 3

To work the Angled stripes block

6 Make a 30cm (12in) square block and a 20cm (8in) right-angled triangle from random strips of fabric, including some that have been pieced together (see page 26). Mark, then cut off a 22cm (9in) triangle from the bottom left corner of the square (fig 4). Sew a dark

strip, 32 x 5cm (13 x 2in), to the long edge of the first triangle, then stitch it onto the square. The cut portion can be used elsewhere on the rug.

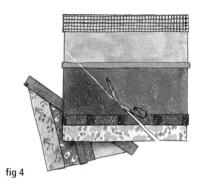

fig 4

To make the Random strips blocks

7 Make these two blocks by joining, cutting and re-assembling random strips of fabric (see page 26) into two 30cm (12in) square blocks.

To work the Little house block

All the seam allowances for this block should be pressed away from the white patches so that the dark blue fabric does not show through the lighter cloth.

To cut out

2 A, 1 C, 1 F, 2 G, 2 H, 1 J & 2 K in dark blue
1 D, 2 E, 1 I, 1 L, 1 M & 1 N in white
1 B in red

To make up the Little house block

8 Sew one A to either side of the door B, then sew C to the top edge to make the gable. Match the bottom left corner of D to the bottom right corner of the block and stitch together along the straight edge as far as the seam allowance. Pivot D so that it lies along the diagonal edge of C and stitch to the end (fig 5). Clip the seam allowance and press the seam away from D.
9 To make the windows, sew one E to either side of F, then add one G to each outside edge. Join the two H strips to the top and bottom of the block. Sew one edge of I to the bottom edge of the roof

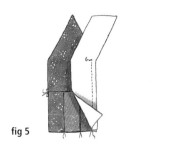

fig 5

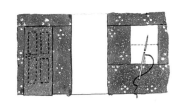

fig 6

fig 7

J, then join the other edge to the window block (fig 6). Join D to the windows and roof, pivoting as before.

10 Join the two chimneys K to either side of L (fig 6), then sew to the top edge of the roof. Add on M and N to finish the block, pivoting at the angle and clipping the allowance. Stitch the outline of the door panelling and the window panes by hand or machine (fig 7).

To work the Basket of scraps block

Also known as flower basket, this design is just one of the many traditional basket blocks. As a variation, the 'petals' could be cut from four different fabrics.

To cut out

1 B & 1 D in red
1 A, 1 E & 1 G in dark blue print
2 C, 1 F, 1 H & 2 I in red-and-white print

To make up the block

11 Join A to B, then set one of the C triangles into the right angle. Sew in two stages, each from the corner to the outside edge, stitching along the seam allowance. Join D, E and the second C in

the same way to make the mirror image. Sew together along the centre seam and set in square F at the corner.

12 Join G to background triangle H along the diagonal, pinning the seam if necessary. Sew G across the base of the petals, then set in the two I rectangles to complete the block (fig 8).

To make up the rug top

13 Sew extra strips of fabric around each of the blocks, to make them all up to 30cm (12in) square. The motifs do not have to lie centrally within the squares. Join the blocks together in three rows of three. Sew three patterned border strips and one short blue strip to two opposite sides of the patchwork square and trim. Stitch the remaining two border strips to the long edges, then press.

To work the quilting

14 Assemble the patchwork, wadding and backing fabric following the method given on page 43. Machine quilt around the square outline of each block, then around the main shape of each motif (see page 45).

fig 8

fig 9

To finish off

15 Trim the wadding and backing fabric so that they are 2.5cm (1in) smaller all round than the patchwork. Tack under a 12mm (½in) turning around the blue border, then fold the hem to the back. Pin, then slip stitch to the backing fabric (fig 9).

log cabin throw

The log cabin quilt, with its connotations of the pioneering homestead, has been a favourite design since the mid-nineteenth century. The orange squares are said to represent the hearth at the centre of the household and the paler areas the firelight, whilst the dark areas are the shadows cast by the flames. Although it may appear complicated at first glance, the patchwork is built up by simply sewing narrow strips of fabric around a square. Rotary cutting and machine stitching make this a quick method of piecing. The basic blocks are all identical – the dramatic effect comes from the way in which they are arranged and the combination of contrasting shades. The secondary pattern of diamonds within the design is emphasized by lines of quilting, and the border is decorated with a free-quilted trailing vine.

fig 1

fig 2

You will need

for a throw 1m (39in) square
Scraps and remnants of light and dark
    fabrics, totalling approximately
    50cm x 1m (20 x 40in) each
25 x 40cm (10 x 15in) dark orange
20 x 80cm (8 x 32in) dark floral print
15 x 60cm (6 x 24in) pale sage
50 x 85cm (20 x 36in) purple
110cm (44in) square of backing fabric
110cm (44in) square of wadding
Matching sewing thread
Red and purple thread for quilting

To cut out

36 36mm (1½in) squares in dark orange
Approx 16m x 2.5cm (17yd x 1in) strips
    each in light & dark fabric
for the border
4 4.5 x 76cm (1¾ x 33in) in dark floral
4 4.5cm (1¾in) squares & 4 11.5cm (4½in)
    squares pale sage
4 11.5 x 83cm (4½ x 33in) strips in purple

To make the patchwork

1 Start the first round by machining a strip of light fabric along the top edge of one square (fig 1). The seam allowance throughout is 6mm (¼in). Trim the strip in line with the side of the square and press the seam away from the centre. Sew a second light strip down the length of the right-hand edge, trim and press (fig 2), then stitch dark strips to the length of the bottom and left-hand edges.

2 The following rounds must be joined in the same order to build up the pattern correctly: fix a small safety pin to the top of the square, so you will always know where to sew the first strip (fig 3). Complete the block by adding another three rounds of two light and two dark strips (fig 4), trimming and pressing each piece as it is sewn. Make 36 blocks in total as described above.

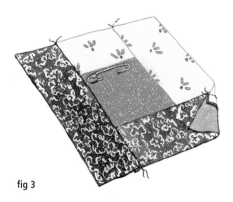

fig 3

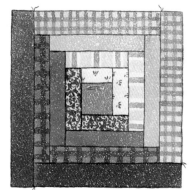

fig 4

3 Lay out the completed squares in six rows of six, changing the direction of the blocks to form a pattern of large diamonds (fig 5). Sew together into rows of six blocks and press the seams to one side, then join the rows. Press and square off the edges if necessary.

To work the quilting

5 Tack together the three layers (see page 43). Outline quilt the inner border. Using a chalk pencil, mark a diagonal grid across the patchwork following the lines between the light and dark strips. Quilt these lines using red thread.

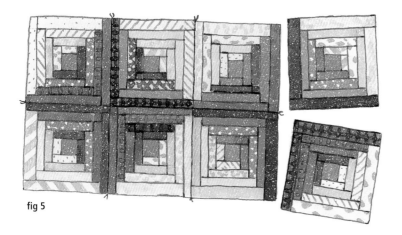

fig 5

fig 6

To make the border

4 With right sides facing, pin one side of the patchwork to a dark floral strip, easing it to fit as necessary. Machine stitch in place, leaving a 6mm (¼in) seam allowance, then sew a second strip to the opposite side. Sew a small green square to each end of the two remaining strips and pin them to the patchwork, matching the seams at the corners. Stitch and press. Attach the purple strips and large green squares in the same way.

Following the quilting diagram (fig 6), mark a curving line along each wide border strip and draw in a series of leaf shapes to make a vine design. Quilt the design in purple thread.

To finish off

6 Trim the wadding to 1m (39in) square. Turn under a hem of 1cm (⅜in) around the border and tack it over the wadding, mitring at the corners. Turn the surplus backing fabric so that it is 3mm (⅛in) smaller than the wadding, and slip stitch it to the border (fig 7). Finally, outline quilt the two sides of the green squares.

fig 7

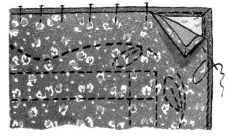

flying geese quilt

The rows of repeated triangles that make up this design are reminiscent of the skeins of migrating birds which give the quilt its traditional name. The lively sense of movement within the geometric arrangement comes from a skilful balance of colour and pattern: the large triangles are cut from a wide selection of brightly printed cottons and set against a background of plain blues and shades of red. The basic motif is quick to sew, and the straight lines that join the blocks and sashing bands make this an ideal project for machine piecing.

You will need

for a quilt 215 x 222cm (86 x 89in)
Remnants of assorted prints totalling
    at least 90cm x 2m (36 x 80in)
90 x 114cm (36 x 45in) mid blue
1m x 114cm (40 x 45in) red stripe
75 x 114cm (30 x 45in) dark blue check
40 x 180cm (16 x 72in) light blue
    sheeting
50 x 114cm (20 x 45in) red
25 x 114cm (10 x 45in) dusky pink
12 x 114cm (5 x 45in) black-and-white
    check
114cm x 5m (45in x 5½yds) backing fabric
265cm (106in) square of wadding
matching sewing and quilting threads

To cut out

(see page 103 for templates)
184 A in assorted fabrics
368 B in mid blue
for the sashing strips
16 3.5 x 175cm (1½in x 70in) in red stripe
16 2.5 x 175cm (1 x 70in) in dark blue
    check
7 5 x 175cm (2 x 70in) in light blue
for the border strips (1 strip of each)
25 x 230cm (10 x 92in) in red
11 x 230cm (4½ x 92in) in dusky pink
5 x 230cm (2 x 92in) in black-and-white
    check
5 x 230cm (2 x 92in) & 2.5 x 230cm
    (1 x 92in) in dark blue check
for the backing fabric
150cm (60in) square

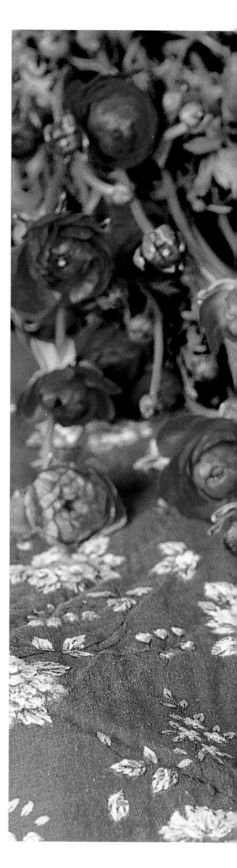

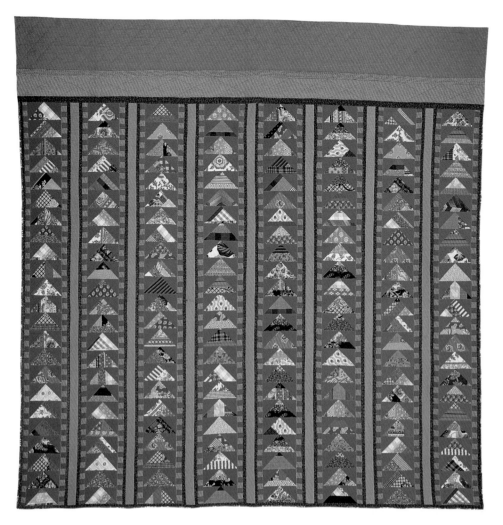

To make up the patchwork

1 Sew the base of B to the upper left edge of A (fig 1). Press the seam allowance towards the small triangle. Sew a second B to the right edge, and press the seam (fig 2), making a rectangular block.

2 For each of the eight triangle strips you will need 23 blocks. To make the strips, sew the blocks together across the long edges and press the seams towards the large triangles (fig 3).

3 Make the sashing bands by sewing a dark blue strip to each red strip. Sew one of these to each edge of a light blue strip, so that the red lies on the outside, and press so that the seam allowances lie away from the dark blue strips (fig 4).

fig 4

4 Assemble the quilt top by sewing the sashing bands between the triangle strips. You may find that each patchwork strip is a slightly different length, so pin each one to the sashing band before stitching, and ease in the fullness as necessary.

5 For the top border, join together the pink, black-and-white check, red and the wider of the two dark blue strips, leaving a seam allowance of 1cm (⅜in). Sew this along the top edge of the quilt; there will be an overlap at the edges, so trim off the surplus fabric in line with the edges of the patchwork. Sew the narrow dark blue strip to the lower edge and trim (see fig 5).

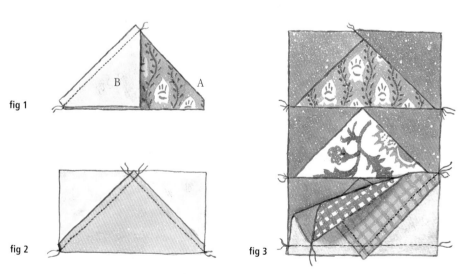

fig 1

B   A

fig 2

fig 3

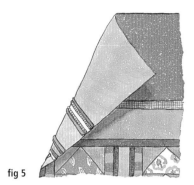

fig 5

To work the quilting

6 Press the quilt top and backing out flat and tack the wadding in place, then attach the top layer (see page 43).

7 Work a line of red quilting stitches along each edge of the dark blue strips, then sew the sinuous lines down the centre of the pale blue strips with blue thread. Outline quilt each triangle. On the top border, mark and stitch a double grid of 5cm (2in) squares across the red strip and a row of 18cm (7in) diamonds along the dusky pink band (fig 6).

8 This basic quilting will secure the layers, but you can fill in the blocks with extra stitching. Instead of the outline stitch, sew a series of parallel lines 1cm (⅜in) apart on each of the small triangles, and work a 2cm (¾in) grid over the large triangles.

To finish off

9 Trim the wadding to 1cm (⅜in) larger all round than the quilt top. Trim the backing so that it is 2cm (¾in) larger than the wadding. Fold under 1cm (⅜in) all round the backing, then slip stitch to the right side of the quilt to bind the raw edges.

fig 6

white quilt

Women of previous generations devoted long hours to embroidering household linen. Many of these beautifully decorated cloths, mats and napkins survive – but few of us now use them for their original purpose. You can recycle an antique piece – and give it a new lease of life – by making it the centrepiece of a quilt. Use this exquisite bedcover as your inspiration: the tablecloth has been set against a white hand-quilted background to emphasize the delicate stitchery. No two old tablecloths will be the same, so adapt the design and colours as you wish. The instructions and measurements below are for a double quilt. If you would prefer to work on a smaller scale, use a traycloth or dressing-table mat as your starting point and give it a simple patchwork border of plain or printed patchwork squares.

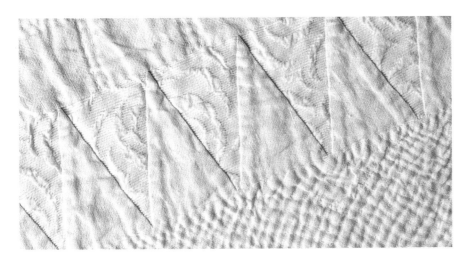

fig 1

You will need
for a quilt approx 2m (80in) square
Square embroidered cloth
40 x 114cm (15 x 45in) textured white fabric, such as cotton piqué
2m x 114cm (2¼ yds x 45in) white linen
50 x 114cm (20 x 45in) yellow cotton print
1m x 114cm (40 x 45in) yellow cotton check
4m x 114cm (4¼yd x 45in) white cotton for backing
215cm (86in) square of cotton domette wadding
White sewing and quilting threads
Paper for templates

To cut out
for the centre panel
Wash and press the tablecloth. Cut off the hem and trim to 111cm (44½in).
You may need to add extra strips of linen to the four sides to make up the size

for the square frame
88 A in piqué
96 A in linen
4 B in yellow print
for the corners
Make a paper template for the corner pieces by cutting a right-angled triangle with two sides measuring 118cm (42in) (length a). Draw a 13cm (5in) vertical line in from each point and cut off the resulting triangles, leaving you with the shape in fig 1
for the border
4 6 x 205cm (2 x 82in) strips & 8 C in yellow print
4 8 x 205cm (3 x 82in) bias strips in yellow check
for the backing
215cm (86in) square of cotton

To make up the quilt top
1 The patchwork frame for the centre panel is made up of alternate linen and piqué triangles A, joined at the corners with yellow 'kites' B. Sew together four strips, each of 22 piqué and 24 linen triangles. Join one B piece to the left edge of each strip and press the seams to one side (fig 2).

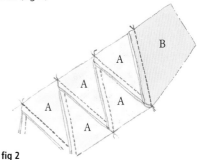

fig 2

fig 3

2 With right sides facing, pin one strip to each edge of the centre, easing as necessary. Stitch 6mm (¼in) from the edge, then join the kites to the adjacent triangles. Add a corner piece to each side, seam the short edges and press. For placement diagram see fig 3.

To work the quilting
3 Assemble the layers as on page 43. Fig 7 shows how each area is quilted but not the order in which they are worked. Starting from the centre, mark and stitch the small and large grids, then outline quilt the frame. Rule a line 12cm (5in) in from the edge and tack along this mark.
4 The wave quilting pattern which fills the triangles is built up from the corners inwards, using two card templates. Cut a 17cm (7in) radius quarter-circle and a 12cm (5in) radius semi-circle. Draw a line to show the centre of each shape.

5 Mark a 45 degree line across the triangle, dividing it into two halves. Place the quarter-circle template in the corner so that it sits on the tacked line and draw round the curve (fig 4). Lay the semi-circle on the tacked line so that the centre point is on the left end of the first curve. Draw around the top of the template from the bottom left corner to the point where it meets the curve. Repeat five times, then do the same on the opposite side (fig 5).
6 Start the second row in the corner. Line up the quarter-circle template so that the half-way mark matches the diagonal line and draw around it. Draw a row of four semi-circles on each side, making sure that they lie parallel to the tacked line. Mark the third row in the same way, then fill in the remaining space with a quarter-circle (fig 6).

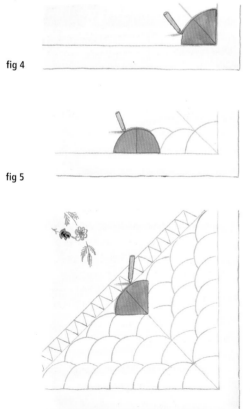

fig 4

fig 5

fig 6

fig 7

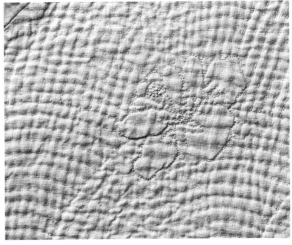

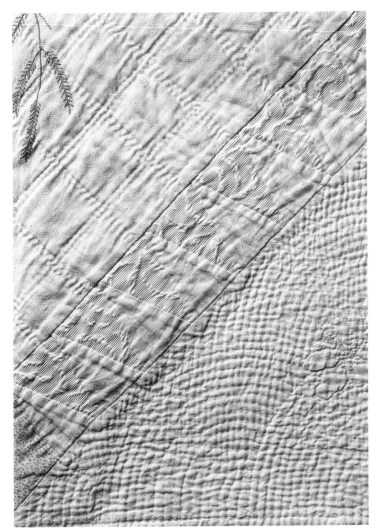

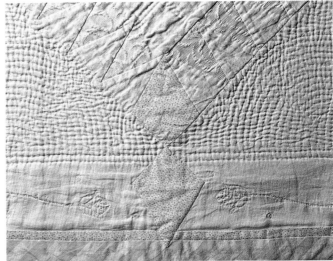

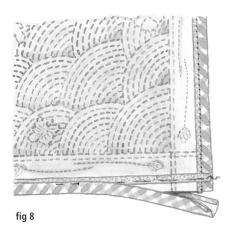

fig 8

7 The waves are broken up with outline quilted flowers (see fig 7), based on the embroidered roses. Draw six of these in each corner. Work the quilting in the order that the pattern was drawn. Quilt each wave by stitching along the outside curve, then working a series of concentric lines 1cm (⅜in) apart to fill the shape. You may prefer to draw them in at first, but with practice you can work by eye.

8 Work two rows of quilting, 1 cm (⅜in) apart along the line marked by the tacking. Fill in the border with outline quilted floral motifs, again based on the embroidery. Trim the quilt to 2m (80in) square.

To finish off

9 Press the narrow border strips in half. Tack one along the first side, so that the cut edges lie 2cm (¾in) in from the edge. Press under 1cm (⅜in) at each edge of a wide strip, then press in half. Pin over the narrow strip to enclose the raw edges (fig 8), then slip stitch to the quilt at the back and front. Do the same on the other sides, overlapping and neatening the corners at the back.

10 Press under 6mm (¼in) around each of the C kite shapes. Appliqué one opposite each patchwork kite and one in each corner (see fig 3).

Piecing by hand

Hand patchwork is an enjoyable and fulfilling technique to practise. As you tack your fabric shapes over their backing papers and stitch them together to create a new textile, you will find yourself becoming involved in an absorbing process that is part of a continuing needlecraft tradition.

It will take time to complete your patchwork this way. As with hand quilting, you should let yourself become immersed in the process of sewing. Work at your own pace and remember that speed is not your main criterion. The oversewn seams are not intended to be an imitation of machine piecing; the softer look that your stitches produce lends charm and individuality to the finished piece.

How to piece by hand

Hand-stitched patchwork involves several stages. A series of templates is cut out from paper, to the exact size of the pieces that make up the design. Fabric shapes, slightly larger than the templates, are folded and tacked over the papers, which are then stitched together. The final appearance of the finished piece will depend on how accurately the papers are cut out. The sharp angles may not meet up exactly when you make your first star, but with experience you will learn how to ease and manipulate the seams so that the patches fit together precisely, like the pieces of a jigsaw.

Preparing the backing papers

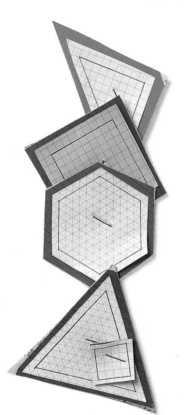

Almost any firm, thin paper can be used as backing – magazine pages, typing paper or brown wrapping paper are all suitable, but anything heavier is too inflexible and will blunt the needle as you sew. Keep the weight of the paper constant throughout one project; using different paper thicknesses will alter the proportions of the shapes and the way you stitch.

Draw up the templates. Use graph paper for squares and right-angled triangles and isometric paper for hexagons and 60 degree diamonds. Follow the given measurements carefully and use a sharp 2H pencil and a ruler. Cut out each shape roughly, then cut three or four pieces of backing paper to approximately the same size. Staple them all together and cut along the pencil line with a craft knife and metal edged ruler (fig 1). Do not use scissors: the blades make the layers splay out as they cut, so the papers will not be identical. Take out the staple with a staple remover. Cut out as many papers as you need to start work. If you are making up a design built up from repeated shapes, the backing papers can be unpicked and re-used. Other motifs are made up from several different pieces, each of which needs its own paper.

Cutting out the fabric
The fabric pieces do not have to be cut out as accurately as for machine piecing: the paper template is cut exactly to size, so this gives the patch its shape. A margin of approximately 1cm (⅜in) should be allowed around each template; this is slightly more than the machined seam allowance and includes the fabric that is lost in turning. The weight of the fabric can affect the width of the seam allowance, so allow slightly more for a thicker cloth. Hold the template against the fabric, following the grain line, and cut out the shape roughly with scissors. Use this piece as a guide for bulk cutting further pieces. If the pattern on your chosen fabric forms part of the finished design, you will have to cut out each shape individually to make sure that stripes lie parallel with the edge and motifs are centred (fig 2).

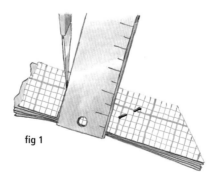

fig 1

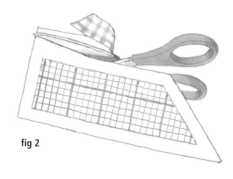

fig 2

Covering the papers

Place the backing paper centrally onto the fabric shape and secure with a few tacking stitches. Always make sure that the knot is on the right side and finish off with a backstitch so the thread can be unpicked easily. Fold over each edge in turn and tack (fig 3). Do not mitre corners of less than 90 degrees as this will make the points bulky; the surplus fabric will be lost on the wrong side.

approximately 40cm (16in) long – any more and it will tangle or break. Hold the pieces right sides together, so that the two edges to be joined line up exactly, and secure the thread at one end. Oversew the seam, picking up just a few threads on each side without stitching through the paper (fig 4). Finish off by working a few stitches in the opposite direction and snipping the thread. Stitch size is a matter of personal

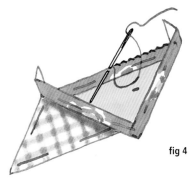

fig 4

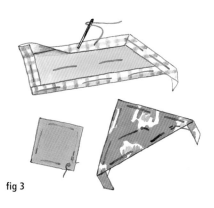

fig 3

Oversewing the seams

When the pieces are sewn together, the thread will show through slightly on the right side. Although you do not have to match it exactly, try to use a light colour for light fabrics and vice versa. Thread your needle with a piece of cotton

preference and can vary between 8 and 12 stitches per 2.5cm (1in). Thread several needles at a time and keep them to hand in a pincushion so you don't loose the rhythm of stitching (you can also do this to save time when you are quilting by hand).

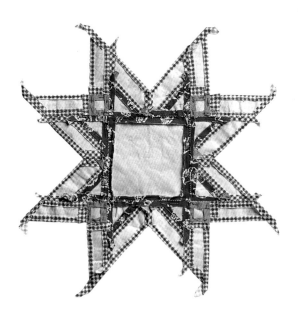

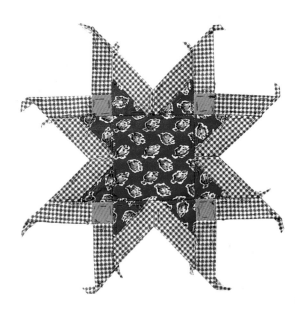

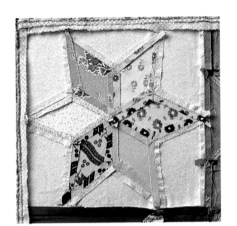

Building up the design

The project instructions all include a diagram showing how to assemble each block, but the order in which the pieces are joined is less critical than with machine piecing. As soon as each piece is surrounded by patches on each side you can carefully remove and re-use the backing papers. This makes the work more manageable, especially when you are working on a large piece. When the motif or block is complete, press lightly at back and front and unpick the remaining papers.

Making a six-point star

Ensuring that the points meet exactly can be tricky, so hand piecing is the best way to make these stars. Join the diamonds in two sets of three, matching up the points carefully. With right sides facing, hold the two pieces together so that the centres lie directly opposite each other and sew from the middle out to each side in turn. Set in the background pieces between the points, by sewing each one from the centre outwards (fig 5).

Sewing curved seams

Joining two curved pieces is not as complicated as it may appear, but you will need to make the tacking stitches closer together than usual so that the fabric lies close along the edge of the papers. For an edge with an outside (convex) curve, you should gather the seam allowance slightly as you tack it down (fig 6). On a sharp inside (concave) curve you may need to make tiny nicks along the edge of the surplus fabric to within 6mm ($\frac{1}{4}$in), and stretch it slightly as you secure it to the template (fig 7).

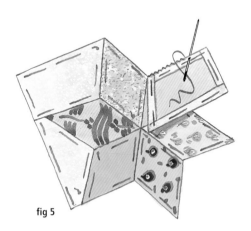

fig 5

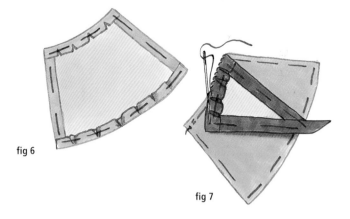

fig 6

fig 7

album panel

The three blocks that make up this charming country-style hanging incorporate all the shapes most commonly encountered in hand-pieced patchwork: the squares, strips and triangles that make up the Sailing Boat and the Ohio Star motifs have angles of either 45 or 90 degrees, while the Six-point Star is made up from sharp-pointed diamonds which meet in the centre. The straight seams of the border strips are machine stitched. You may wish to make up the hanging in fabrics to match a particular colour scheme.

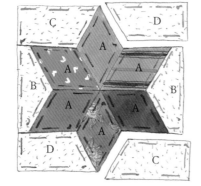

fig 1

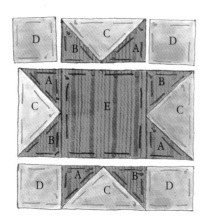

You will need:
for a hanging 28 x 72cm (11 x 29in)
for the Six-Point Star
22 x 25cm (9 x 10in) light blue floral
7 x 12cm (3 x 5in) each of 6 different
   red fabrics
for the Ohio Star
15 x 20cm (6 x 8in) red stripe
15 x 30cm (6 x 12in) pale blue
for the Sailing Boat
18 x 30cm (7 x 12in) red check
15 x 17cm (6 x 7in) light blue floral
8 x 23cm (3 x 9in) floral stripe
for the borders
10 x 25cm (4 x 10in) brown
5 x 71cm (2 x 28in) green
5 x 71cm (2 x 28in) blue
10 x 33cm (4 x 13in) in 2 checks
10 x 71cm (4 x 28in) in 2 more
   checks
for the ties
15 x 50cm (6 x 20in) in 2 checks or
   stripes
28 x 72cm (11 x 29in) backing
   fabric
Tacking thread
Matching sewing thread
Backing paper

To cut out the border strips & ties
These all include a seam allowance of
1cm (⅜in)
4 4 x 22cm (1½ x 9in) in brown
1 4 x 69cm (1½ x 27in) in green &
   also in blue
2 8 x 30cm (3¼ x 12in) each in a
   different check
2 8 x 69cm (3¼ x 27in) each in a
   different check
4 7 x 60cm (3 x 24in), 2 each in a
   different check

The patchwork templates are given at the back of the book. Cut out a backing paper for each shape and add a seam allowance of 1cm (⅜in) onto each fabric piece. Tack all the fabric to the papers.

To cut out the Six-point star block
6 A each in a different shade of red
2 B, 2 C & 2 D in light blue floral

To make up the block
1 Lay out the six diamonds A so that they form a balanced arrangement and stitch together to form a star shape (see page 67). Sew the two B pieces into the triangular spaces on both sides. Complete the square by joining one C and one D to the top and bottom of the star (fig 1).

To cut out the Ohio star block
4 A, 4 B & 1 E in red
4 C & 4 D in pale blue
If you are using a striped fabric, you will need to change the direction of some of the small triangles so that the stripes run in the same direction across the star. Cut two As and two Bs along the grain as marked, then turn the templates through 90 degrees to cut the other four triangles.

To make up the block
2 Make four rectangles by joining one A and one B to either side of each large triangle C. Sew two of these along the sides of the large square E, with the points facing outwards. Stitch a small square D to either end of the remaining rectangles to make two strips, then sew these to the top and bottom of the centre block, making sure that the points face outwards (fig 2).

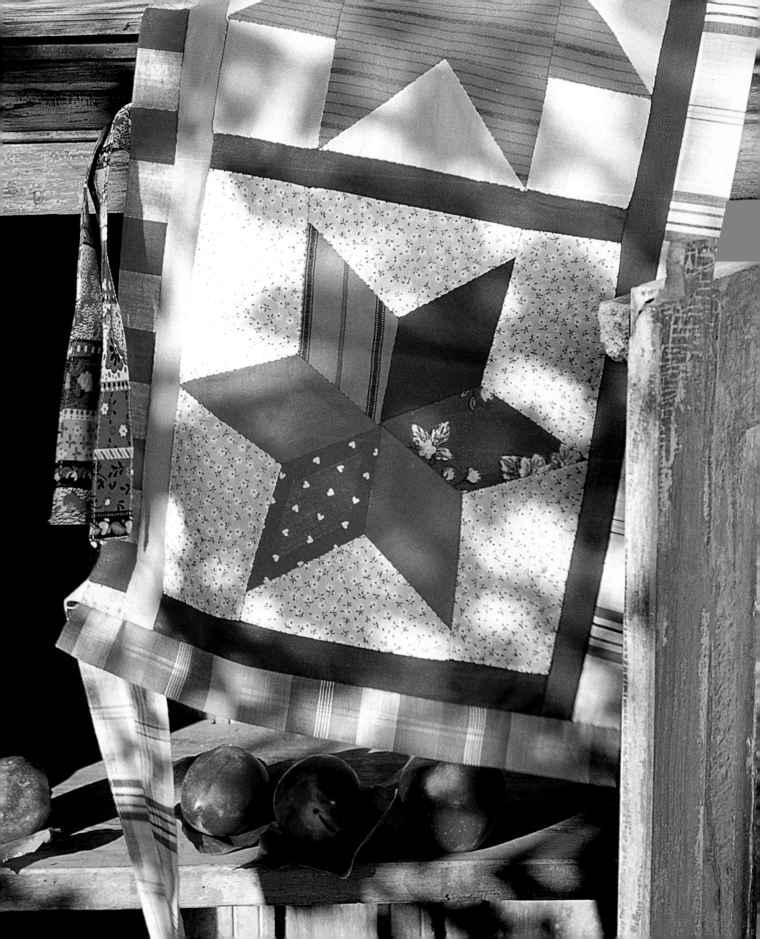

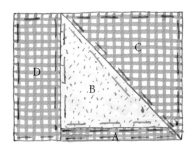

fig 3

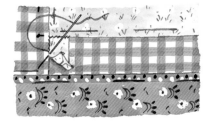

fig 4

To cut out Sailing boat block

1 A, 1 C, 1 D, 1E & 1 F in red check
1 B in light blue floral
1 G in floral stripe
1 2 x 2.5cm (¾ x 1in) rectangle in light
   blue floral for the mast

To make up the block

3 Join the narrow strip A to the bottom edge of the sail B, then sew the large triangle C along the diagonal edge. Sew rectangle D to the other side of B. Sew triangles E and F to either side of the base of the boat G (fig 3), then join the two blocks to form a square. Unpick the backing paper from background piece A. Finger press a 6mm (¼in) turning around the mast. Appliqué to the left side of A, in line with the sail (fig 4).

To make up the hanging

4 When the three blocks are complete, unpick the papers and press out the turnings around each edge. Pin a brown border strip along each side of the six-point star and the sailing boat blocks, making sure that the points match up with the seam line. Sew in place, then pin and stitch these blocks to either side of the eight-point star. Trim the ends of the strips so that they are in line with the blocks, if necessary, and then press the seams flat.

5 Join a long check border strip to the green and the blue strips, and sew to the top and bottom edges of the hanging, again matching the points. Press the seams open and trim the corners (fig 5). Sew the remaining border strips to the two sides and trim. Press the seams open, then press under the seam allowance along each edge.

6 With wrong sides together, pin the backing fabric to the hanging so that there is an equal margin of border strip all round. Turn the surplus fabric to the back and pin in place. Slip stitch down, making a small mitre at each corner (fig 6).

To make the ties

7 Press under 1cm (⅜in) along each edge of one tie strip, then with right sides facing outwards, press in half lengthways. Tack together, then machine stitch all round, 3mm (⅛in) from the edge (fig 7). Make up the other three ties in the same way. Fold each in half widthways and slip stitch to the top back edge, so that each is in line with a brown border strip.

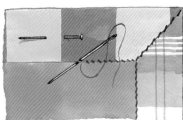

fig 6

fig 5

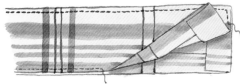

fig 7

pattern pieces

These sample pieces started life as colour and design experiments, effectively illustrating the kaleidoscope of different results that can be achieved by working within a circular format. They provide a good way to practise hand-piecing techniques, including curved seams, and to get used to working with backing papers and smaller pieces of fabric. Although the patterns may appear complex at first glance, they can all be broken down into separate elements which are easy to put together. The finished pieces have been quilted, so make ideal tablemats; you could stitch a mixed or matching set, or explore the effects of making up one motif in several different colourways.

The templates for all the mats are at the back of the book. Following the outlines, cut one backing paper for each piece of your chosen design. Add an extra 1cm (⅜in) all round when cutting out the fabric shapes. Tack the fabric to the papers.

Each mat measures approximately 25cm (12in) in diameter.

Hexagon star

The points of this star are made up from two striped triangles, which create a chevron pattern when sewn together. If you prefer to use a plain fabric for the points, they can instead be cut from one equilateral triangle.

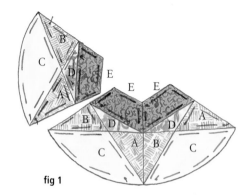

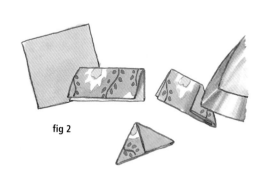

fig 1

You will need
18 x 20cm (7 x 8in) dusky pink check
15 x 20cm (6 x 8in) pale blue
25 x 30cm (10 x 12in) cream
15 x 20cm (6 x 8in) burgundy print
25 x 30cm (10 x 12in) mustard print
30cm (12in) square of backing fabric
30cm (12in) square of polyester wadding
matching sewing thread
dark red thread for quilting
backing paper for patchwork pieces

To cut out
6 A & 6 B in dusky pink check
6 C in cream
6 D & 1 9cm (3½in) square in pale blue
6 E in burgundy print
18 6cm (2½in) rectangles in mustard print
1 23cm (9½in) circle from wadding
1 27cm (10¾in) circle from backing fabric

To work the patchwork
1 Six identical segments are joined together to make the circle, and a round of triangular points is added to the outside edge. Each segment is made by sewing triangles A and B to either side of C, then joining the small triangle D to E. Stitch the other two sides of D to the large triangles. Sew all six together to make a ring (fig 1), press and remove the backing papers.

2 Make the 16 points by folding each mustard square in half, then pressing the top corners to the centre (fig 2). Arrange them around the outside edge of the patchwork with the folded sides uppermost. Adjust so that they are evenly spaced and the raw edges overlap the wadding by 6mm (¼in). Pin in place (fig 3), then sew to the patchwork with dark red running stitch.

To make up the mat
3 Turn under and tack a 1cm (⅜in) hem around the backing fabric. Tack the blue square to the centre of the wadding, then pin the wadding between the backing and the patchwork, making sure that they line up exactly. Slip stitch the hexagonal opening to the blue fabric behind, then slip stitch the backing fabric to the reverse side of the mat.

To work the quilting
4 Outline quilt the hexagon and the six-sided shape around it, the small blue triangles and the large triangles formed by pieces A and B. Stitch a series of concentric curved lines 6mm (¼in) apart in the cream areas. Finish by working three rows of stitches across the centre hexagon to divide it into triangles.

fig 2

fig 3

Rose window

This combination of cotton fabrics in blue, white and the distinctive shade of crimson known as 'Turkey Red', is typical of traditional American patchwork.

You will need

25cm (10in) square white
25cm (10in) square red
20 x 45cm (8 x 18in) mid blue
25 x 30cm (10 x 12in) dark blue
30cm (12in) square of polyester wadding
30cm (12in) square of backing fabric
Matching sewing thread
Black thread for quilting
Backing paper for patchwork pieces

To cut out

8 A in white
8 A in red
16 B & 1 8cm (3in) circle in mid blue
16 C in dark blue
1 23cm (9½in) circle from wadding
1 27cm (10¾in) circle from backing fabric

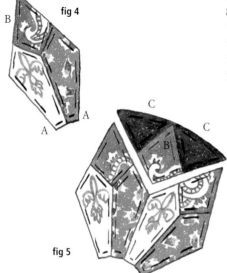

fig 4

fig 5

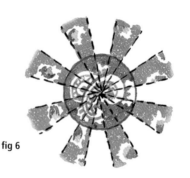

fig 6

To make the patchwork

1 The design consists of a series of pentagons and triangles. Start by joining B to the top right edge of one white A, then sewing on a red A (fig 4). Make eight of these blocks, then join the side seams together.

2 Sew one C to either side of the remaining Bs to form eight triangles. Stitch one of these into the right-angled space between the points of the first block (fig 5). Complete the circle by joining the remaining blocks in the same way. Press, then remove backing papers.

To make up the mat

3 Tack the small blue circle to the centre of the wadding, then assemble and tack the three layers as in step 3 of the Hexagon Star. Slip stitch the centre opening to the blue circle behind it.

To work the quilting

4 Outline quilt each piece, then stitch a line from the edge of each piece A to the centre of the mat (fig 6).

Dresden plate

This flower-shaped design is an ideal way of using up your smallest fragments of fabric. Its name – inspired by the bright patterns found painted on old china – makes it an ideal choice as part of a table setting.

You will need

12 9 x 12cm (3½ x 5in) scraps of
 different fabrics
12cm (5in) square of cream
28cm (11in) square of lightweight
 backing fabric
25cm (10in) square of wadding
Matching sewing thread
Yellow thread for quilting
Backing paper for patchwork pieces

To cut out

1 A from each fabric

To make the patchwork

1 Tack the fabric to the backing papers, then take time to arrange the pieces so that they form a pleasing, balanced arrangement of colour and pattern. Sew together into a circle (see fig 7), then press before removing the papers.

fig 7

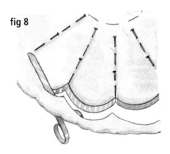
fig 8

backing fabric in place and trim to 6mm (¼in) outside the edge (fig 8).

3 Tack under the edges to that it is the same size as the patchwork, clipping the corners for a neat edge (fig 8). Join the front and backing together with a round of small running stitches. Slip stitch the centre opening to the cream fabric.

To work the quilting

4 Rule and stitch an 8mm (⅜in) grid across the centre circle, then following the lines given on the template, quilt the inside of each 'petal'. As a variation, the quilting can be worked in backstitch.

To make up the mat

2 Tack the cream fabric to the middle of the wadding, then pin on the patchwork. Turn over and trim the wadding back to 6mm (¼in) inside the edge. Pin the

Clarice's circle

The bright glazes and bold patterns of Clarice Cliff's 1930s studio pottery are the influences behind this dynamic Art Deco design.

You will need
12 x 25cm (5 x 10in) dark orange
12 x 25cm (5 x 10in) yellow
10 x 18cm (4 x 7in) tangerine
15 x 20 cm (6 x 8in) purple
18 x 20cm (7 x 8in) turquoise
15 x 20cm (6 x 8in) lilac
30cm (12in) square of polyester wadding
30cm (12in) square of backing fabric
Matching sewing thread
Orange and purple thread for quilting
Backing paper for patchwork pieces

To cut out
4 A in dark orange
4 A in yellow
4 B in tangerine
4 C & 12 4cm (1½in) squares in purple
4 D in lilac
4 E in turquoise
23cm (9½in) circle of wadding
26cm (10¼in) circle of backing fabric

To work the patchwork

1 The circle is made up of eight slices in two different patterns. To make the first four, sew the dark orange A to E and

E to D (fig 9). For the other slices, sew yellow A to B and B to C by stitching 1cm (⅜in) at each end of the seam (fig 10).

2 Make the 12 points by folding each purple square in half, then pressing the top corners to the centre (fig 11), and insert three into each of the spaces, with the folded sides uppermost.

3 Pin the points in place so that they overlap slightly, then slip stitch the top of B to hold them in place. Working from the back, sew the lower edge of A to the back of the triangles. Join the alternate segments to make a circle. Press and remove the backing papers.

To make up the mat

4 Join together the three layers as for step 3 of the Hexagon Star.

To work the quilting

5 Work diagonal double rows of purple quilting, 1cm (⅜in) apart, across each D, an 1cm (⅜in) orange grid across B and parallel lines 6mm (¼in) apart along each dark orange A.

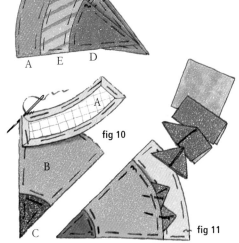
fig 9
fig 10
fig 11

Mariner's star

The crisp blue-and-white striped fabric used for the outer triangles of this 12-pointed star gives a nautical feel to the compass-like design.

You will need
20 x 30cm (8 x 12in) cream
18 x 20cm (7 x 8in) blue stripe
8 x 12cm (3 x 5in) mustard
18cm (7in) square light blue
18cm (7in) square dark blue
16 x 18cm (6 x 7in) dark blue stripe
30cm (12in) square of polyester
 wadding
30cm (12in) square of backing fabric
Tacking thread
Matching sewing thread
Blue thread for quilting
Backing paper for patchwork pieces

To cut out
6 A in mustard
6 B in light blue stripe
6 C & 6 D in cream
6 E in light blue
6 F in dark blue
6 G in dark blue stripe
1 23cm (9½in) circle from wadding
1 27cm (10¾in) circle from backing
 fabric

To make the patchwork
1 This circular motif is made up from six matching 'slices'. Join A to B along the curved seam, easing it to fit as you stitch. Sew C and D to either side of B, matching the points at the bottom edge so that the tip of the triangle projects beyond the curve (fig 12). Sew E and F to the block, then make another five segments in the same way.
2 Join two blocks together along the side seam. Sew the first border piece G along the curved edge, then to the sides of the triangle points. Finish the circle by adding the remaining segments and border pieces in the same way (fig 13). Press lightly, then remove the papers.

To make up the mat
3 Turn under and tack a 1cm (⅜in) hem around the backing fabric, easing the fullness as you stitch. Pin the wadding between the backing and the patchwork, making sure that they line up exactly, then sew together around the edge with a round of small running stitches. Sew lines of tacking stitch, 5cm (2in) apart across the mat or safety pin the layers together.

To work the quilting
4 Outline quilt the striped and mustard triangles, the diamonds formed by the blue triangles and the outside edge of the cream areas. Rule an 8mm (⅜in) grid across these areas, parallel to the sides of the striped triangles, and stitch in blue.

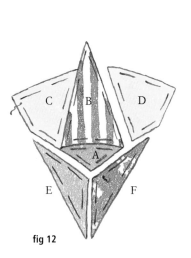

fig 12

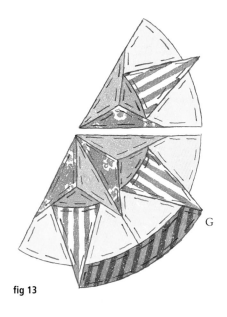

fig 13

basket cot quilt

Basket motifs have always been popular with the quilt makers and there are many different variations. Some are filled with fruit or flowers, whilst others – like these – have curved handles. The unusual arrangement of the four blocks that make up the cot cover gives a geometric look, which is emphasised by the patchwork stripes and bold use of colour. The washable polyester wadding has a tactile, slightly puffy quality, and the cotton fabrics will withstand the wear and tear of daily use.

You will need

for a quilt 68cm (27in) square
18 x 28cm (7 x 11in) yellow
25 x 30cm (10 x 12in) pale blue chambray
25 x 45cm (10 x 18in) blue-and-white stripe
80 x 90cm (32 x 36in) dark blue chambray
50 x 70cm (20 x 28in) white
76cm (30in) square of backing fabric
76cm (30in) square of lightweight Flameproof polyester wadding
Tacking thread
Backing paper
Matching sewing thread
White and yellow thread for quilting

To cut out

Use the templates and measurements on page107. The border pieces L, M & N include 6mm (¼in) seam allowances. Cut backing papers for the pieces A, B, C, D, E, F, H, I, J & K and allow an extra 1cm (⅜in) margin when cutting out the fabric shapes. Tack all the basket and background pieces except F to their respective papers

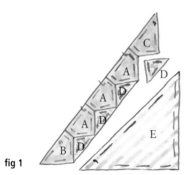

fig 1

for the baskets
12 A, 4 B, 4 C, 8 J & 3 3.5 x 27cm (1⅜ x 10½in) strips in pale blue
16 D & 4 3.5 x 27cm (1⅜ x 10½in) strips in yellow
4 F in blue-and-white stripe
13 3.5 x 23cm (1⅜ x 9in) strips in dark blue
14 4.5 x 23cm (1¾ x 9in) strips in white
for the background
1 H, 4 K & 4 N in white
2 G & 2 I in blue-and-white stripe
for the border
4 M in white
4 N & 4 L in dark blue

To make the baskets

1 For each of the four basket bases, join three As together along the shortest edges and add one B and one C to the ends of the row. Sew 4 Ds into the triangular spaces between them. Sew the longest side of triangle E to the edges of the small triangles (fig 1).
2 The top sections of the basket blocks are cut from dark blue and white strips. Starting with white, sew alternate blue and white pieces together, leaving a seam allowance of 6mm (¼in). Press seams towards the blue fabric. Using template F as a guide and adding on approx 1cm (⅜in) all round, mark and cut out four large triangles (fig 2). The apex of each triangle lies at the centre of a blue stripe.
3 The handles are cut on the bias, from fabric that has been joined in the same way. Sew together the seven yellow and blue pieces, starting with yellow. Press the seams to one side, then mark four 3 x 26cm (1¼ x 10in) strips at an angle of 45 degrees (fig 3). Cut out and press

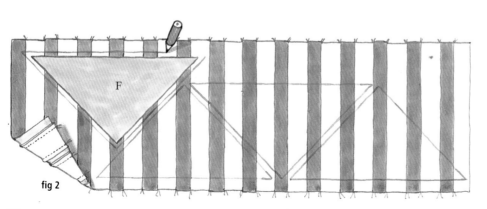

fig 2

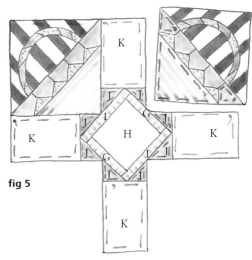

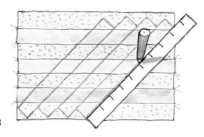

fig 3

fig 4

fig 5

under a 6mm (¼in) turning at each long edge, then gently press each handle into a curve. Pin each one to an F triangle, making sure that the shapes are all the same. Slip stitch in place (fig 4), then tack the fabric to the backing papers. Join to the top edge of the basket bases.

4 Make the centre by stitching a G strip to either side of the white square H, then add an I strip to the remaining sides. Sew two J triangles to each side of the square to form a cross, then add a K rectangle to each arm of the cross. Complete the centre panel by sewing one basket square into each corner space (fig 5).

To make the border

5 Machine stitch the diagonal edges of two blue strips L to either side of a triangle M along the seam line, then join them together along the short edges. Do the same with the other two Ls and with the four longer N pieces. Press the seams away from the white fabric.

6 Press the patchwork lightly and unpick the papers. Press out the seam allowances along the outside edges. With right sides facing, pin the two short border pieces to opposite sides of the square. Line the triangles M up with the rectangles K, and match the seam line of the border strips to the crease line around the centre panel. Machine stitch, then sew on the other two borders in the same way. Press the seam allowances towards the outer edge.

To work the quilting

7 Tack the wadding and backing in place (see page 43). Outline quilt G and I with yellow thread and quilt the motifs and border 'in the ditch' using white thread.

To finish off

8 Trim the backing fabric and the wadding to 68cm (27in) square. Tack under 1cm (⅜in) around the outside edge of the quilt top and turn the surplus fabric to the back. Pin, then slip stitch down, squaring off the corners.

79

antique rose quilt

This is a mosaic patchwork which is made from four interlocking shapes, arranged to create an overall repeating pattern. The subtle effect of this is enhanced by the choice of materials; the five different fabrics are in closely toning colours and similar shades which give a muted, watercolour look to the quilt. This quilt is made unmistakably contemporary by the unusual combination of woven Indian check and faded rose-patterned chintz.

You will need
for a quilt 155 x 185cm (62 x 74in)
1m x 114cm (36 x 45in) blue floral print
1m x 114cm (36 x 45in) white floral print
60 x 114cm (24 x 45in) blue-and-white check
80 x 114cm (32 x 45in) dusky pink check
50 x 150cm (20 x 60in) pink striped fabric for border
4m x 114cm (2yd x 45in) backing fabric
1 55 x 185cm (62 x 74in) wadding
Matching sewing and quilting threads
Backing paper for patchwork pieces

To cut out
Draw the templates from page 108 onto card to use as a guide for cutting out the fabric, allowing an extra 1cm (⅜in) margin around each shape. Cut the backing papers to the exact size of the templates: you will need about half as many as there are fabric pieces. Tack the fabric to the papers and re-use them as you go.
72 A & 71 D in red-and-blue check
154 B in blue floral
156 B in white floral
168 C in pink check
for the border
88 E in blue floral
88 E in white floral
2 13 x 120cm (5 x 47in) and
   2 13 x 150cm (5 x 59in) strips in pink stripe
for the backing fabric
1 55 x 185cm (62 x 74in)

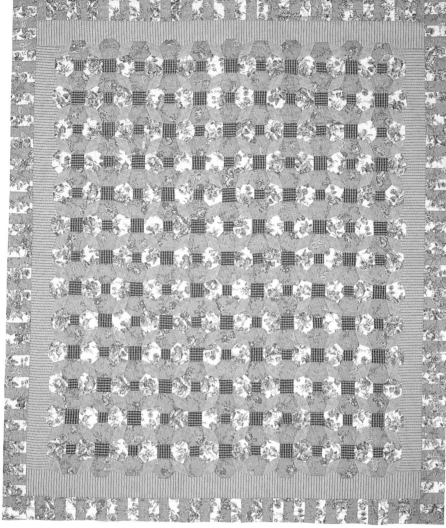

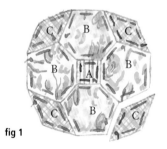

fig 1

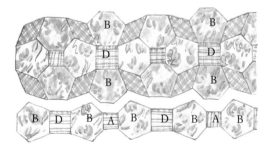

fig 2

To make the patchwork

1 The main block is made by sewing two blue and two white hexagons B around a small square A to form a cross, then stitching a diamond C into each corner space (fig 1). Make 42 blocks.

2 Make the 'bow-tie' shapes which link the main blocks by stitching blue hexagons to either side of a large square D. You will need 35 of these. Make seven rows, each of six blocks and five bow-ties (fig 2).

3 The rows of main blocks and blue 'bow-ties' are linked with lines of white 'bow-ties', which are made in the same way. Sew them together in six lines containing six blocks, interspersed with small squares (fig 2). Join the alternate rows of main blocks and white 'bow-ties' to make the quilt top, starting and finishing with a main block row. Press the quilt top, then remove the remaining backing papers.

To make the border

4 The patchwork is hand stitched to the inner border. Mark a 2cm (¾in) line along one long edge of each blue border strip. Starting 2cm (¾in) from the end, pin the long sides of the patchwork to the long border strips, following the marked line. Trim the surplus fabric at each end to 1cm (⅜in) and then press under. Slip stitch the patchwork to the border. Pin and stitch the short sides in the same way.

Slip stitch onto the long sides where they overlap at the corners (fig 3). Square off as necessary.

5 Make four strips of alternate blue and white rectangles for the striped edge. Leaving a 6mm (¼in) seam allowance, machine stitch two rows of 38 Es and two rows of 50 Es. Press the seams to one side. Sew one short strip to each short edge of the quilt and press. Join the long strips to the other sides. Press and square off as necessary (fig 4).

fig 3

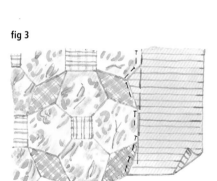

fig 4

To work the quilting

6 Sandwich the layers together following the technique on page 43. Starting from the centre, outline quilt each of the patchwork shapes and stitch a series of parallel lines across the inner border.

To finish off

7 Trim the wadding and backing so that they are 4cm (1½in) smaller than the quilt top. Turn under and tack a 12mm (½in) hem all round, then fold the surplus fabric to the back of the quilt. Pin and slip stitch down, making neat square corners. Finally, outline quilt each floral rectangle.

dresden plate quilt

The Dresden Plate pattern originated in 1930s America, when it would have been made up in small-scale dress prints on a white background. For this fresh reworking of the design, a selection of stripes, gingham, floral and Provençal prints has been put together with a wide yellow check and three strong plain colours. Orange stars have been added to break up the sashing bars and the shapes within the festive border echo the main motif. The round 'plates' and the stars are hand pieced and appliquéd to the quilt, whilst the rest of the pieces are machine stitched.

You will need

for a quilt 150 x 210cm (60 x 84in)
120 x 114cm (48 x 45in) yellow check
50 x 114cm (20 x 45in) of 8 different
    patterned fabrics for the 'plates'
75 x 114cm (30 x 45in) orange
35 x 114cm (14 x 45in) light blue
40 x 114cm (16 x 45in) lilac
170 x 230cm (68 x 92in) wadding
3.5m x 114cm (4yd x 45in) backing fabric
backing paper
tacking thread
matching sewing thread
thread for quilting

To cut out

Cut backing papers for the A and F pieces. Add on an extra 1cm (⅜in) all round when cutting the fabric, then tack to the papers. All the other pieces are joined by machine and include a seam allowance of 6mm (¼in).
225 A (approx 28 in each fabric)
15 29cm (11½in) squares in yellow check
20 B, 20 C, 16 D & 8 E in lilac
22 5.5 x 24cm (2¼ x 9½in) & 16 8 x 24cm (3¼ x 9½in) strips in light blue
144 F in orange
58 G (8 in each of 6 fabrics, 10 in 7th fabric)
54 H in orange
4 I in floral print

To make the blocks

1 Each 'plate' is made up from 15 A pieces, three of one fabric and two each of six others. Arrange them in a circle so that the matching pairs lie opposite each other and sew together along the sides (fig 1). Press and unpick the papers. Pin the patchwork centrally to a yellow check square, making sure that it lies flat, and slip stitch in place around the outer and inner edges.

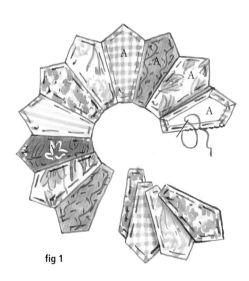

fig 1

To assemble the quilt top

2 Join the 'plates' together into five rows of three blocks. Sew one B piece to each end of ten narrow blue strips and press the seams towards the Bs. Stitch and press the 20 C pieces to ten of the wide strips in the same way. Join three blocks together by sewing the narrow strips between them, then sew a wide strip to each outside edge. Press the seams towards the blue strips (fig 2).

3 Sew together four Ds alternating with three narrow blue strips. Press the seams towards the D pieces (fig 3). Pin and stitch this band to one long edge of a row of blocks, and press the seam allowance towards the band. Make another three bands in the same way, then pin and stitch the rows together. Press all the seams towards the bands.

4 Join the remaining wide blue strips into two bands, each made up of four Es and three strips (fig 4). Press as before, then sew one strip to each end of the quilt top.

To make the stars

5 The 24 orange stars are made by sewing together six diamonds F. Press each one, then remove the backing papers. Pin one star to each lilac area following the photograph as a guide, and slip stitch in place (fig 5).

fig 2

fig 3

fig 4

To make the border

6 Make the two long borders by sewing together 18 G pieces, alternating with 17 orange Hs (fig 6). Pin and stitch in place, then press the seam allowance towards the centre. The borders for the short sides are each made up of two rows of 11 Gs and 11 Hs, starting with an H. Sew one I piece to the end of each short row, then pin and stitch to the quilt, matching the corners. As you sew the border together, you may find that there is some extra fullness, which gives it a slightly ruffled appearance. This will disappear when it is quilted.

To work the quilting

7 Tack the patchwork top, wadding and backing fabric together (see page 43). Following fig 7 as a guide, outline quilt around each shape within the plates and along the lines of the check print. Outline quilt the stars and the 'tie' shapes around the edge and work close parallel lines of stitches at a 45 degree angle across the border strips.

To finish off

8 Trim the wadding so that it is 1cm (⅜in) smaller all round than the quilt top, then cut the backing fabric to the same shape as the patchwork. Tack under a 6mm (¼in) turning around the quilt top. Turn under and tack the edge of the backing fabric, so that it lies 3mm (⅛in) from the folded edge of the quilt top. Clip into the corners so that the surplus fabric will lie flat. Pin and tack, then slip stitch the two layers together (fig 8). Finish off by outline quilting the border pieces.

fig 5

fig 6

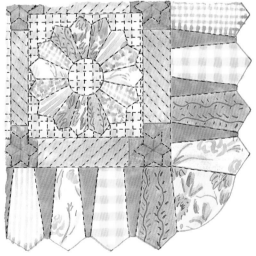

fig 7

fig 8

harlequin quilt

The inspiration for this nostalgic bedcover is the 1920s era, when chintz roses and harlequin diamonds were the fashion for ladies' boudoirs. The floral centrepiece, however, uses the Broderie Perse appliqué technique which dates from the eighteenth century, when imported fabrics were rare and precious. Individual motifs are cut out from a printed design, rearranged and sewn into a new pattern in a textile version of paper découpage. The surface of the quilt is stitched with a garland and grid patterns, and it is bordered with a wide band of patchwork in multicoloured prints.

You will need

for a quilt 200 x 277cm (80 x 111in)
for the quilt centre
140 x 114cm (56 x 45in) mid blue
25 x 114cm (10 x 45in) dark blue
40 x 114cm (16 x 45in) dress-weight fabric with large-scale floral pattern
60 x 114cm (24 x 45in) red print
50 x 114cm (20 x 45in) dark green
for the border
250 x 114cm (100 x 45in) multicoloured geometric
1m x 114cm (40 x 45in) lilac
60 x 114cm (24 x 45in) each of 7 different prints
220 x 300cm (90 x 120in) wadding
580 x 114cm (232 x 45in) backing fabric
66cm (26in) square of paper
Pencil, string and drawing pin
Backing paper
Tacking thread
Matching sewing thread
Thread for quilting

To cut out

for the quilt centre
100 x 130cm (39 x 51in) in mid blue
2 5 x 100cm (2 x 39in) & 2 5 x 136cm (2 x 55½in) strips in dark blue
2 12 x 106cm (5 x 42in) & 2 12 x 159cm (5 x 64in) strips in red print
4 8 x 20cm (3 x 8in), 2 8 x 110cm (3 x 44in) & 2 8 x 130cm (3 x 52in) strips in dark green
for the border
Allow an extra 1cm (⅜in) around each shape when cutting out the fabric.
208 A & 68 B in geometric print
100 A in lilac
approx 59 A in all of the 7 prints
46 C in assorted prints

To make the quilt centre

1 Make a circular template 66cm (26in) in diameter by folding the paper into quarters. Tie the string to the point of the pencil. Pin the other end to the folded corner and, keeping the string taut and the pencil upright, draw an arc. Cut out along this line. Fold the blue rectangle into four and press lightly. Pin the circle to the fabric, matching the creases, and draw around it (fig 1).
2 Cut a selection of motifs from the floral print, leaving a 6mm (¼in) margin around each one. Clip the curves and points, fold under and tack the surplus fabric (fig 2). Arrange the shapes within the circle, approximately 5cm (2in) from the edge. Join buds, flowers and leaves to form sprigs. Pin, then stitch in place.

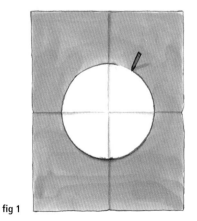

fig 1

fig 2

3 Machine stitch two dark blue strips to the top and bottom edges, leaving a seam allowance of 1cm (⅜in), then add the longer strips to the sides. Sew on the red print strips in the same way, press seams towards the blue fabric. Mark points 15cm (6in) from the end of each side and 9cm (3½in) from the end of the top and bottom. Rule a diagonal at each corner and cut off the triangles (fig 3).

4 Sew a short green strip across each corner, then sew the other strips to the side and top edges of the rectangle. Press seams towards the green fabric. Tack the backing to the wadding, then tack the quilt centre to the centre front.

To make the border

5 Lay the quilt flat and arrange A, B and C shapes around the top using the placement above as a guide. The sides are five and a half diamonds wide, the top and bottom are three and a half diamonds deep. The inner and outer edges are made up of geometric print shapes, and the sides are bordered with triangles made up from one A and two Cs. Swap the pieces around until the prints are distributed evenly, store and label them carefully so they can be stitched in the right order.

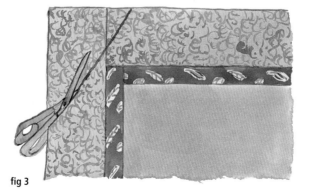

fig 3

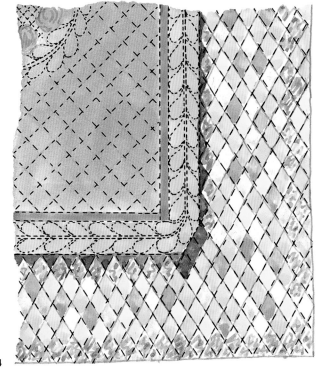

fig 4

To assemble the quilt top

6 Iron the border. Unpick the papers and press the seams along the edges. Place it around the centre panel so the points of the diamonds are equidistant from the orange band. Tack the border down, then slip stitch the zigzag edge to the quilt.

To work the quilting

7 Following fig 4, mark a second line 6mm (¼in) outside the centre circle. Draw the inner and outer garland shapes D and E around the parallel lines (see page 45) and rule a 12mm (½in) grid in the circle. Rule two lines 6mm (¼in) apart around the centre of the orange band and mark the F shapes along either side. Quilt over the lines. Outline quilt each diamond.

To finish off

8 Trim wadding to same size as quilt top. Cut off surplus backing fabric, leaving 5cm (2in) margin at each side. Fold the margin to quilt front, making a 1cm (⅜in)turning all round. Slip stitch down.

stars & diamonds quilt

This beautiful quilt is a true heirloom piece. Floral prints in fine lawn, shirting and a pale turquoise blue cotton blend together to create a colour scheme which evokes a flower-filled garden. The pattern of stars, lozenges and hexagons is a 'one-patch' design made up from a single repeated shape – a small diamond motif. The patchwork centre and corner motifs are hand pieced and the borders are sewn on by machine, then quilted.

You will need

for a quilt 217 x 242cm (87 x 97in)
120 x 114cm (48 x 45in) each of yellow floral and dark paisley
170 x 114cm (68 x 45in) red floral
40 x 114cm (16 x 45in) each of 5 other fabrics: 2 stripes, 2 dark florals & 1 light paisley
120 x 114cm (48 x 45in) striped shirting
220 x 114cm (88 x 45in) light blue
50 x 114cm (20 x 45in) dark red print for binding
238 x 263cm (95 x 105in) wadding
6m x 114cm (6½yd x 45in) backing fabric
Backing paper
Tacking, sewing and quilting threads

To cut out

for the quilt centre
This is made up of over 2,000 pieces, so instead of preparing all the pieces at the outset, it is easier to cut and tack one block at a time. Allow an extra 1cm (⅜in) around each template when cutting out the fabric.
for the border strips
4 5 x 20cm (2 x 8in), 2 5 x 203cm (2 x 81in) & 2 5 x 295cm (2 x 120in) in red floral
2 16 x 203cm (6½in x 81in) & 2 18 x 253cm (7 x 101in) in light blue

for the corner motifs
24 A in dark floral
8 B in light blue
4 D in yellow floral
4 D in dark paisley
8 E in stripe
2 8 x 250cm (3 x 100in) & 2 8 x 300cm (3 x 120in) strips in dark red for binding
238 x 263cm (95 x 150in) backing fabric

To make the quilt centre

The quilt centre is made up of rows of large hexagons which are linked together with diamonds. Half- and quarter-diamonds are sewn around the four sides to make a rectangle.

To cut out the hexagon blocks

Make 35: each one contains two light blue hexagons and has a border of shirting, but the choice of the other three colours should be different for each block
18 A in shirting
12 A in colour 1
6 A in colour 2
6 A in colour 3
6 A in light blue

To make up the hexagon blocks

1 Sew together six colour 1 As to form a star. Make a hexagon by joining three blue As and sew this between two of the star's points. Sew a second blue hexagon to the opposite side. Make four more hexagons from colours 2 and 3 and sew around the star (fig 1).
2 Stitch a colour 1 diamond into each of the spaces between the hexagons, then complete the block by sewing three shirting As between each projecting diamond (fig 2).

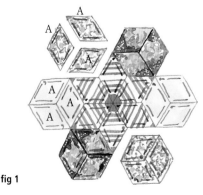

fig 1

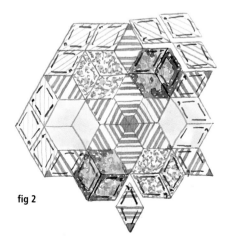

fig 2

93

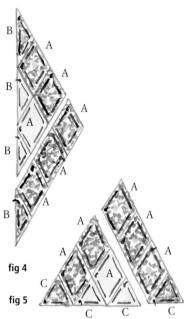

fig 4

fig 5

To cut out the long half-diamond blocks

Make 12: 6 with yellow floral border, 4 with red floral border and 2 with dark paisley border.
1 A & 2 B in light blue
5 A & 2 B in printed fabric

To make the long half-diamond blocks

4 Join two blue Bs to the blue A to make a long triangle. Sew two printed As and 1 B into a row and join to one side. Stitch the other three As and the remaining B together and sew to the other side (fig 4).

To cut out the short half-diamond blocks

Make 8: 4 with yellow floral border and 2 each in red and dark paisley
1 A & 2 C in light blue
5 A & 2 D in printed fabric

To make the short half-diamond blocks

5 Join two blue Cs and the blue A forming a triangle. Sew two printed As and one C into a row and stitch along one edge, then sew the remaining shapes into a row and add to the second edge (fig 5).

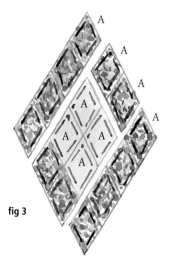

fig 3

To cut out the diamond blocks

Make 24: 12 edged with yellow floral As and 6 each edged with red floral and dark paisley.
4 A in light blue
12 A in printed fabric

To make the diamond blocks

3 Sew together the four blue As to make a diamond. Join two pairs of patterned As and sew to opposite sides of the block. Sew remaining As into two rows of four and sew one to each long edge (fig 3).

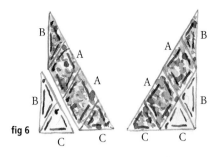

fig 6

fig 7

To cut out the quarter-diamond blocks
Make 4: 2 with yellow border, and 1
    each with red and dark paisley.
1 B & 1 C in light blue
2 A 1 B & 1 C in printed fabric

To make the quarter-diamond blocks
6 Each block is made by joining a light
blue B and C to form a right-angled
triangle and sewing a row of two
printed As, a B and a C to the long
edge. Reverse the direction of two of
the blocks, so that there is one for each
corner of the quilt (fig 6).

To assemble the quilt centre
7 When you have completed all the
blocks, lay the hexagons out in seven
rows of five so that the small blue
hexagons all lie in the same direction.
Place the diamonds between them and
the half- and quarter-diamonds around
the edges (see page 94), using the
photograph as a guide. Rearrange the
shapes until you have a balanced layout.
Sort and label the blocks so that you will
be able to sew them together in the
right order.
8 Join the hexagons into five rows of
seven. Sew the half- and quarter-
diamonds in place along the outside edges
of the first and last rows, then join the
rows together by sewing the diamonds
and half-diamonds between them.
Remove the backing papers and press the
seams outwards at the outside edges.

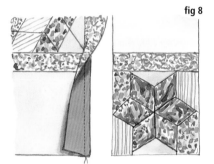

fig 8

To make the border

9 Make each of the four corner motifs by sewing together six As to form a star. Join two Bs to opposite sides, then fill in the top and bottom spaces with two Ds and two Es (fig 7). Unpick the papers, press the edges outwards. Machine stitch a short red strip to one long side of each star and trim to the same length as the patchwork.

10 Join the two 5 x 203cm (2 x 81in) red strips to the two border pieces of the same length, then machine stitch to the top and bottom of the quilt centre. Press the seams towards the red fabric.

11 Sew the long red strips to each side and press the seams outwards. Sew one corner motif to each end of the long border pieces and pin to the sides of the quilt, matching up the red strips.

12 Stitch, then press the seam allowance towards the centre. The corner motifs do not line up with the border pieces, but all the raw edges will be covered by the binding (fig 8).

To work the quilting

13 Tack the quilt top, wadding and backing fabric together (see page 43). Outline quilt each star within the hexagons and the corner motifs, and each A shape inside the large diamonds, and half- and quarter-diamonds. Outline quilt the red border strips, then free quilt the blue borders as shown in fig 9. Make the star template by drawing around a diamond template six times onto a piece of firm paper.

To finish off

14 Trim the wadding and backing fabric so they are the same size as the quilt top. Press under 1cm (⅜in) along each side of the binding strips, then press in half lengthways. Pin, then sew to the short edges of the quilt, slip stitching in place at the front and back. Trim the ends. When binding the other two sides, leave an overlap of 2cm (¾in) at each end. Fold the surplus to the wrong side, turn under the raw edge and slip stitch down (fig 10).

fig 9

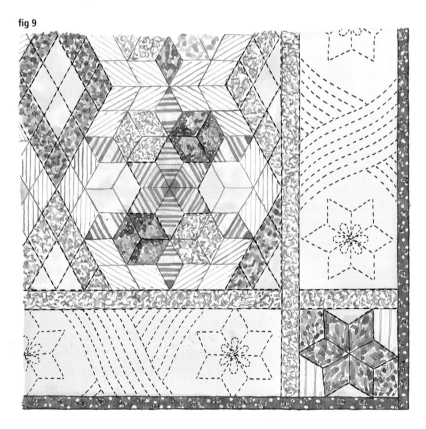

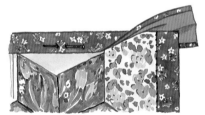

fig 10

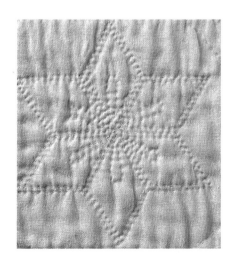

Templates

The templates for all the projects are given on the following pages. Some of them are reproduced at the correct size and can be traced off directly or photocopied at 100%. Others are half-size and will need to be enlarged to 200%.

The templates for all machine-stitched patterns include a seam allowance of 6mm (¼in) (see page 25). For hand-stitched pieces, the shapes given are for backing papers (see page 64). A few projects include both types of template. The arrows indicate the grain line.

A cut 1
cut 1 reversed

b

a

b

c

c

g

B cut 1
cut 1 reversed

a

C cut 1
cut 1
reversed

f

e

d

d

g

toys & trifles

Scottie dog
Enlarge to 200%
on a photocopier

f

e

D cut 1
cut 1
reversed

97

toys & trifles

Victorian boot
Enlarge to 200% on a photocopier

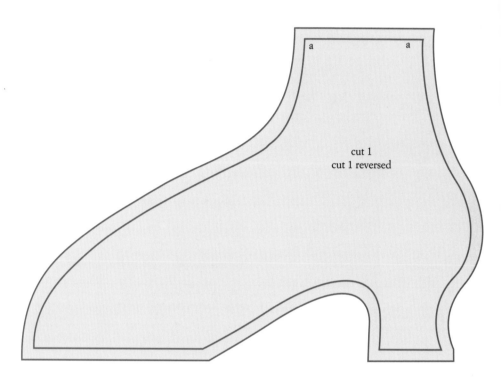

cut 1
cut 1 reversed

Lace-up shoe
Enlarge to 200% on a photocopier

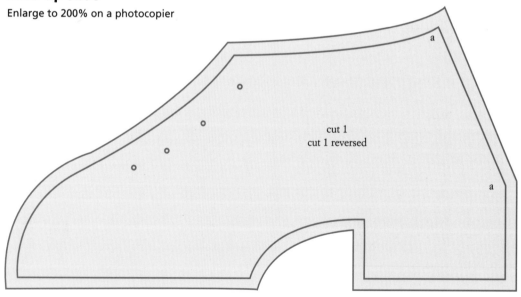

cut 1
cut 1 reversed

simply
stars

These shapes are actual size

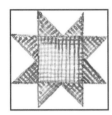

G
cut 4

E
cut 4

F
cut 4

A
cut 32

B
cut 16

D
cut 4

C
cut 16

ohio star throw

These shapes are actual size

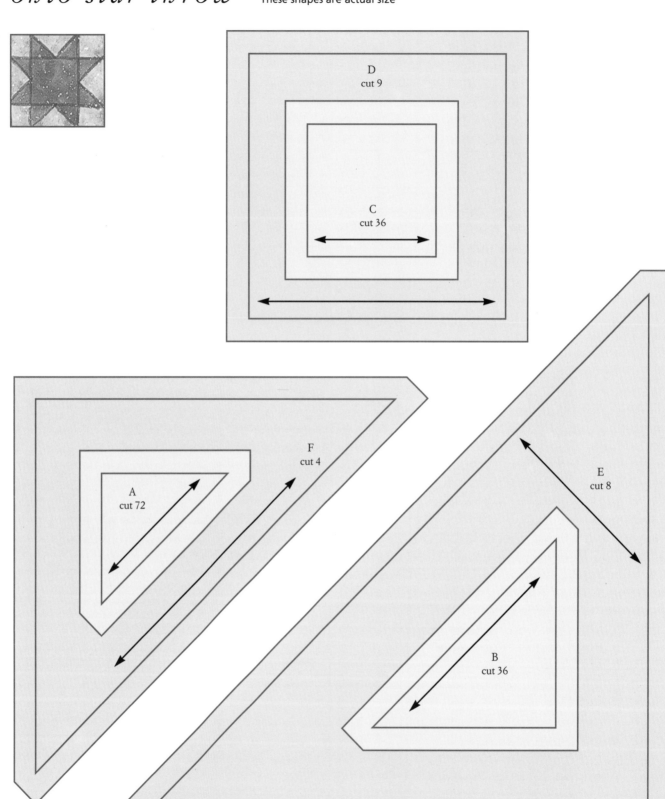

D
cut 9

C
cut 36

F
cut 4

A
cut 72

E
cut 8

B
cut 36

sampler rug

Faceted star
Enlarge to 200%
on a photocopier

Sailing boat
Enlarge to 200%
on a photocopier

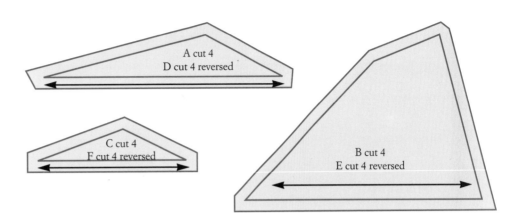

A cut 4
D cut 4 reversed

C cut 4
F cut 4 reversed

B cut 4
E cut 4 reversed

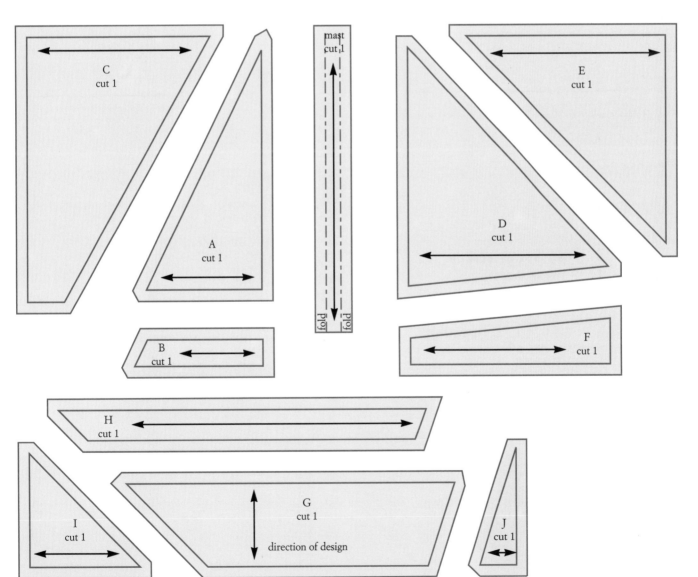

C
cut 1

A
cut 1

mast
cut 1

fold   fold

E
cut 1

D
cut 1

B
cut 1

F
cut 1

H
cut 1

I
cut 1

G
cut 1

direction of design

J
cut 1

101

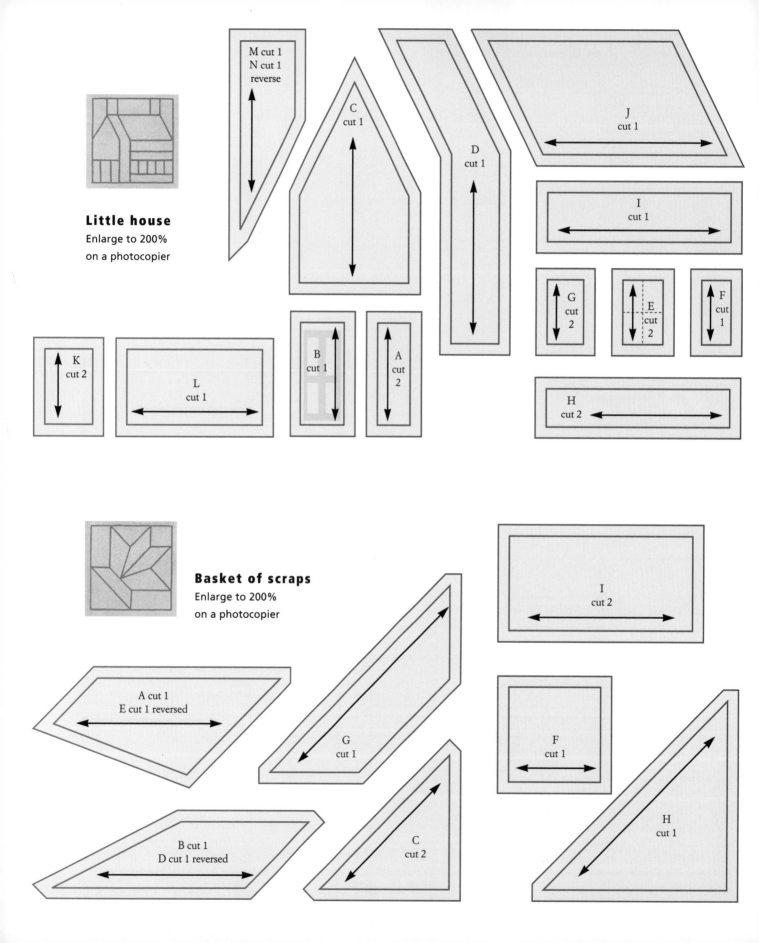

Little house
Enlarge to 200%
on a photocopier

M cut 1
N cut 1
reverse

C
cut 1

D
cut 1

J
cut 1

I
cut 1

G
cut 2

E
cut 2

F
cut 1

B
cut 1

A
cut 2

H
cut 2

K
cut 2

L
cut 1

Basket of scraps
Enlarge to 200%
on a photocopier

A cut 1
E cut 1 reversed

G
cut 1

I
cut 2

B cut 1
D cut 1 reversed

C
cut 2

F
cut 1

H
cut 1

flying geese

These shapes are actual size

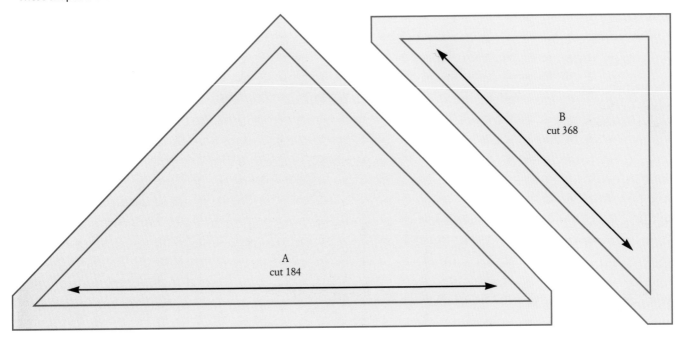

A
cut 184

B
cut 368

white quilt

These shapes are actual size

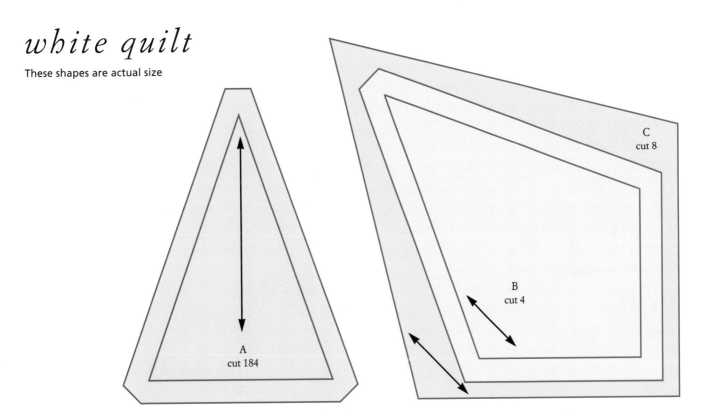

A
cut 184

B
cut 4

C
cut 8

album panel

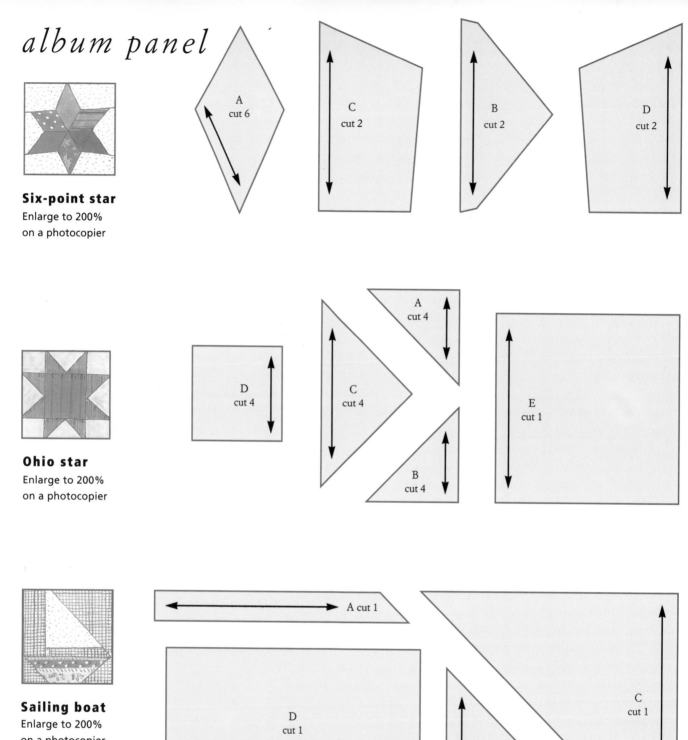

Six-point star
Enlarge to 200%
on a photocopier

A cut 6

C cut 2

B cut 2

D cut 2

Ohio star
Enlarge to 200%
on a photocopier

D cut 4

C cut 4

A cut 4

B cut 4

E cut 1

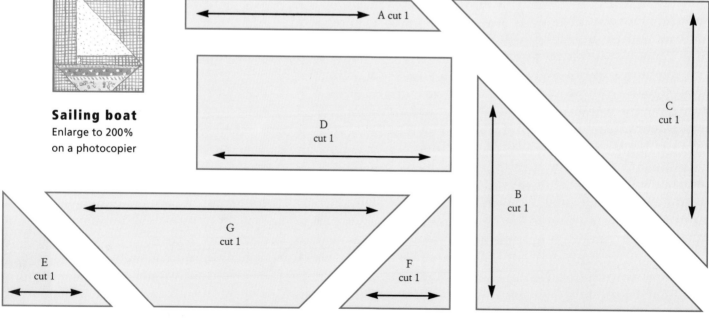

Sailing boat
Enlarge to 200%
on a photocopier

A cut 1

D cut 1

C cut 1

B cut 1

G cut 1

E cut 1

F cut 1

pattern pieces

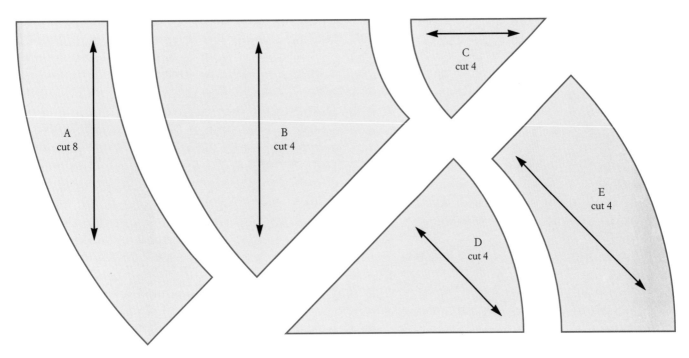

A
cut 8

B
cut 4

C
cut 4

D
cut 4

E
cut 4

Clarice's circle

These shapes are actual size

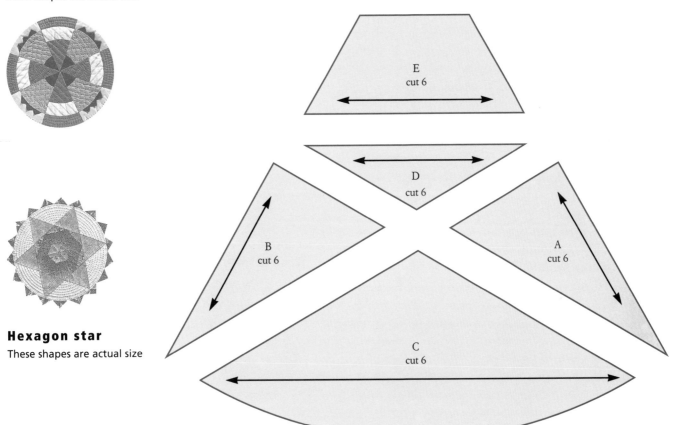

E
cut 6

D
cut 6

B
cut 6

A
cut 6

C
cut 6

Hexagon star

These shapes are actual size

Mariner's star

These shapes are actual size

G
cut 6

B
cut 6

D cut 6
C cut 6 reversed

A
cut 6

F cut 6
E cut 6 reversed

A
cut 11

Dresden plate

This shape is actual size

Rose window

These shapes are actual size

C
cut 16

B
cut 16

A
cut 16

cot quilt Enlarge to 200% on a photocopier

Draw the following templates up on graph paper
G 1 x 12cm (⅜ x 4¾in) (cut 2)
H 12 x 12cm (4¾ x 4¾in) (cut 1)
I 1 x 14cm (⅜x 151/2in) (cut 1)
K 10 x 15cm (4 x 6in) (cut 4)

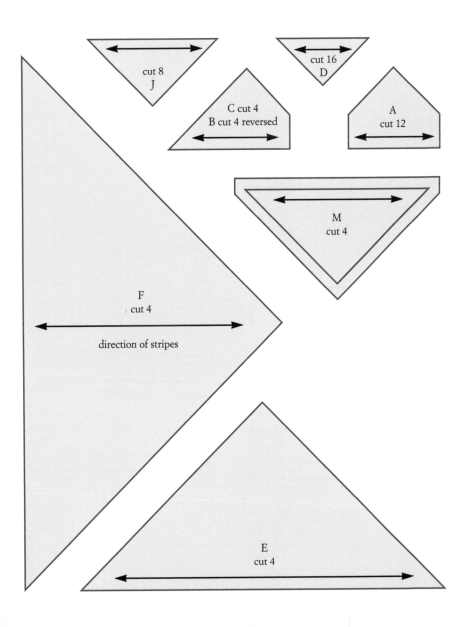

cut 8
J

cut 16
D

C cut 4
B cut 4 reversed

A
cut 12

M
cut 4

F
cut 4
direction of stripes

E
cut 4

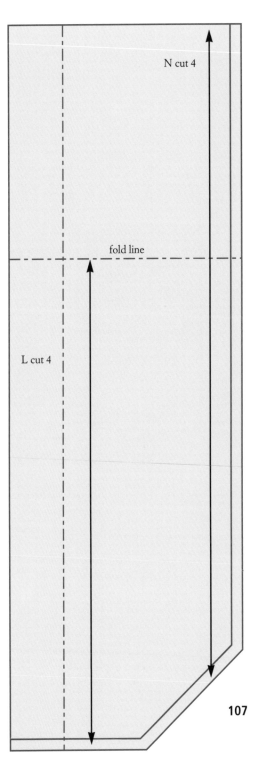

N cut 4

fold line

L cut 4

107

antique rose

Enlarge to 200% on a photocopier

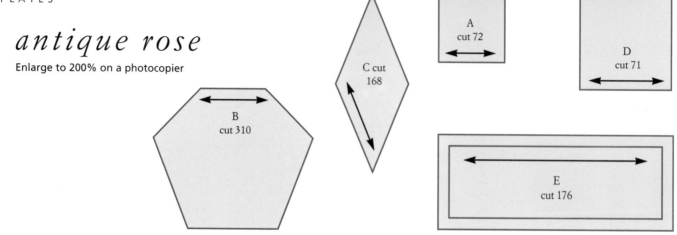

B
cut 310

C cut
168

A
cut 72

D
cut 71

E
cut 176

dresden plate Enlarge to 200% on a photocopier

Draw these templates up on graph paper
B 56 x 38cm (22½ x 15¼in) (cut 20)
C 82 x 38cm (33 x 15¼in) (cut 20)
D 108 x 58cm (43 x 23in) (cut 16)
E 108 x 82cm (43 x 33in) (cut 8)

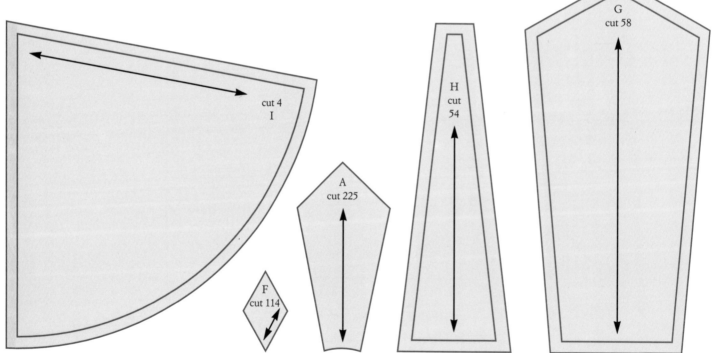

cut 4
I

A
cut 225

F
cut 114

H
cut
54

G
cut 58

harlequin quilt
These shapes are actual size

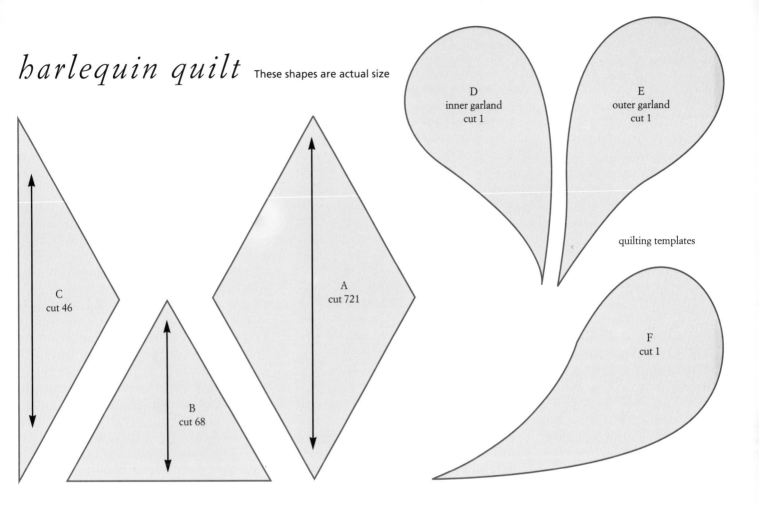

C
cut 46

B
cut 68

A
cut 721

D
inner garland
cut 1

E
outer garland
cut 1

quilting templates

F
cut 1

stars & diamonds
These shapes are actual size

This quilt is made up of over 2,000 pieces.
Cut out the papers and fabric for each block as you come to it

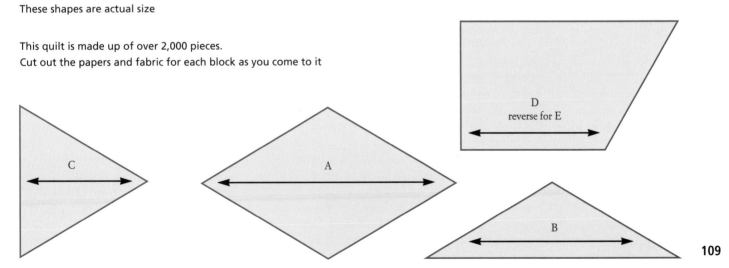

C

A

B

D
reverse for E

index

acknowledgments

Diane Crawford would like to thank everybody who has been involved in creating this book, particularly the editorial and design team at Quadrille: Mary Evans, Jane O'Shea, Nathalie Hennequin and Kathy Seely, whose enthusiasm for the quilts made it possible. To Linda Burgess and Nicky Dowey for their vibrant photographs and Kate Simunek for her beautiful illustrations. Special thanks to Lucinda Ganderton for writing this book and the many hours spent in working out the instructions for the projects. Thanks to Doreen Crawford for teaching me to sew. To Jules for his love and support and finally to Lynne Robinson and Dick Lowther for introducing me to Mary.

Lucinda Ganderton would like to thank Jane and Mary for their creative support, Kathy for her unfailing editorial guidance and patience, Nathalie for her design skills, Kate for interpreting my sketches into such exquisite watercolours, and Diane for her friendship and inspiration.

At Sylvan, we believe writing is among life's most important skills, and we're glad you've chosen our resources to help your child build this crucial knowledge. A successful writer is ready for the world around her, and her creativity will enrich everything she writes; or, she can use these skills to guide her research and effectively communicate what she has learned in school. With these skills, children will be successful in life as well as in school.

At Sylvan, writing instruction uses a step-by-step process with research-based and thought-provoking lessons. With success, students become more confident. With increasing confidence, students build even more success. That's why our Sylvan workbooks aren't like the others; we're laying out the roadmap for learning.

Included with your purchase is a coupon for a discount on our in-center service. As your child continues his academic journey, your local Sylvan Learning Center can partner with your family to ensure that your child remains a confident, successful, and independent learner.

The Sylvan Team

Sylvan Learning Center.
Unleash your child's potential here.

No matter how big or small the academic challenge, every child has the ability to learn. But sometimes children need help making it happen. Sylvan believes every child has the potential to do great things. And, we know better than anyone else how to tap into that academic potential so that a child's future really is full of possibilities. Sylvan Learning Center is the place where your child can build and master the learning skills needed to succeed and unlock the potential you know is there.

The proven, personalized approach of our in-center programs deliver unparalleled results that other supplemental education services simply can't match. Your child's achievements will be seen not only in test scores and report cards but outside the classroom as well. And when he starts achieving his full potential, everyone will know it. You will see a new level of confidence come through in everything he does and every interaction he has.

How can Sylvan's personalized in-center approach help your child unleash his potential?

• Starting with our exclusive Sylvan Skills Assessment®, we pinpoint your child's exact academic needs.

• Then we develop a customized learning plan designed to achieve your child's academic goals.

• Through our method of skill mastery, your child will not only learn and master every skill in his personalized plan, he will be truly motivated and inspired to achieve his full potential.

To get started, included with this Sylvan product purchase is $10 off our exclusive Sylvan Skills Assessment®. Simply use this coupon and contact your local Sylvan Learning Center to set up your appointment.

And to learn more about Sylvan and our innovative in-center programs, call 1-800-EDUCATE or visit www.SylvanLearning.com. *With over 1,100 locations in North America, there is a Sylvan Learning Center near you!*

5th-Grade
Writing Success

Published in the United States by Random House, Inc., New York, and in Canada by Random House of Canada Limited, Toronto.

www.tutoring.sylvanlearning.com

Created by Smarterville Productions LLC
Cover and Interior Photos: Jonathan Pozniak
Cover and Interior Illustrations: Delfin Barral

First Edition

ISBN: 978-0-375-43011-4

Library of Congress Cataloging-in-Publication Data available upon request.

This book is available at special discounts for bulk purchases for sales promotions or premiums. For more information, write to Special Markets/Premium Sales, 1745 Broadway, MD 6-2, New York, New York 10019 or e-mail specialmarkets@randomhouse.com.

PRINTED IN CHINA

10 9 8 7 6 5 4 3 2 1

Contents

Checking your answers is part of the learning.

Each section of the workbook begins with an easy-to-use Check It! strip.

1. Before beginning the activities, cut out the Check It! strip.

2. As you complete the activities on each page, check your answers.

3. If you find an error, you can correct it yourself.

Writing Nonfiction

1

Fact and Fiction

Some people love to write. Some people hate it. No matter how you feel, writing is the best way for you to share all those big ideas in your head. And the world needs your big ideas!

When you stick to the facts, that's NONFICTION. You always have to tell the truth and check your information when you write this kind of story.

FILL IN the blanks with fiction and nonfiction story ideas for each topic.

Topic: Sharks

Fact: _A shark attack survivor telling his terrible story_

Fiction: _A girl getting a pet shark and keeping it in her bathtub_

Topic: Baseball

Fact: _____

Fiction: _____

Topic: Outer Space

Fact: _____

Fiction: _____

Topic: Rock 'n' Roll Music

Fact: _____

Fiction: _____

Actually, you can write *exactly* the *same* stories for both fiction and nonfiction, but in nonfiction, every word has to be true.

✓ Check It!

Page 1

Fact and Fiction

Suggestions:

Topic: Baseball
Fact: The Red Sox winning the World Series
Fiction: A 10-year-old who joins the major leagues

Topic: Outer Space
Fact: The moons of Jupiter
Fiction: A kid who moves to Jupiter with his family

Topic: Rock 'n' Roll Music
Fact: A real-life band on their first worldwide tour
Fiction: A made-up story about a kid who starts a band with his parents

Page 2

Suggestions:
1. Shirley Temple
2. Amelia Earhart
3. George Clooney
4. Franklin D. Roosevelt
5. Marie Curie

Page 3

Suggestions:
1. the sun
2. the 1920s
3. industrial farming
4. global warming
5. the Civil War

Page 4

Suggestions:
1. make a paper airplane
2. make paper flowers
3. braid hair
4. roller blade
5. do a lay-up

1

Fact and Fiction

Some people love to write. Some people hate it. No matter how you feel, writing is the best way for you to share all those big ideas in your head. And the world needs your big ideas!

When you stick to the facts, that's NONFICTION. You always have to tell the truth and check your information when you write this kind of story.

FILL IN the blanks with fiction and nonfiction story ideas for each topic.

Topic: Sharks

Fact: A shark attack survivor telling his terrible story

Fiction: A girl getting a pet shark and keeping it in her bathtub

Topic: Baseball

Fact: _____

Fiction: _____

Topic: Outer Space

Fact: _____

Fiction: _____

Topic: Rock 'n' Roll Music

Fact: _____

Fiction: _____

Actually, you can write *exactly* the *same* stories for both fiction and nonfiction, but in nonfiction, every word has to be true.

✓ Check It!

Page 1

Fact and Fiction

Suggestions:

Topic: Baseball
Fact: The Red Sox winning the World Series
Fiction: A 10-year-old who joins the major leagues

Topic: Outer Space
Fact: The moons of Jupiter
Fiction: A kid who moves to Jupiter with his family

Topic: Rock 'n' Roll Music
Fact: A real-life band on their first worldwide tour
Fiction: A made-up story about a kid who starts a band with his parents

Page 2

Suggestions:
1. Shirley Temple
2. Amelia Earhart
3. George Clooney
4. Franklin D. Roosevelt
5. Marie Curie

Page 3

Suggestions:
1. the sun
2. the 1920s
3. industrial farming
4. global warming
5. the Civil War

Page 4

Suggestions:
1. make a paper airplane
2. make paper flowers
3. braid hair
4. roller blade
5. do a lay-up

Writing Nonfiction

 **Check It!**

Page 5

Suggestions:
1. Reggie Jackson joining the Yankees
2. Surviving the *Titanic* disaster
3. The U.S. hockey team win at the 1980 Olympics
4. Charles Lindbergh's first nonstop flight from New York to Paris
5. The Brooklyn Dodgers move to Los Angeles

Page 6

Suggestions:
1. **Go:**
   - A ski resort, like Big Sky in Montana
   - A local snowboarding supply store
   - A snowboarding club meeting or class

2. **Read:**
   - Magazines for snowboarders
   - Books about snowboarding
   - A snowboarding blog on the Internet

3. **Ask:**
   - An expert snowboarder
   - A snowboard supply specialist
   - A reporter who covers snowboarding competitions

You can write nonfiction stories about tons of different topics, like people, history, nature, and sports. These topics are called GENRES.

When you write a story about a person's life, it's called a *biography*. When you write your own life story, that's an *autobiography*.

READ this story.

Boy on a Board

Tony Hawk got his first skateboard when he was nine years old. Before that, he says, "I was a hyper, rail-thin geek on a sugar buzz." That skateboard changed everything. As he got good at skating, he calmed down, felt better about himself, and thought more about other people. He really started to grow up.

Now, LIST five people you would like to write nonfiction stories about.

1. _____

2. _____

3. _____

4. _____

5. _____

You can also write about science or history to help your readers learn about those topics.

READ these stories.

On the Job at Five

During the Industrial Revolution in the 1800s, factory workers spent 16 hours straight in hot, smelly rooms filled with loud and dangerous machines. A lot of these workers were kids—some as young as five years old. Children were really useful because they had small fingers that could make tiny things like matches or nails. They could also fit inside the chimneys of rich people's houses to clean them.

These kids were helping to support their families, but most adults didn't like the idea. Over time, the government stepped in. Most countries made it illegal for people under the age of about 14 to have a job. However, "most" countries doesn't mean *all* countries. There are some places where little kids still spend their days sewing, farming, or working in factories.

Rotating with Earth

The Earth is rotating under our feet. It's traveling west to east at about 500 miles per hour. So why can't you just go up in a helicopter, hover in one spot for a few hours, and then land in a totally different place? (No, it doesn't work.) See, the Earth takes its atmosphere along for the ride. If it didn't, we'd be in trouble. Imagine a dog hanging its head out of a car window while the car is driving 500 miles per hour down the road!

Now, LIST five history, science, or nature topics you would like to write nonfiction stories about.

1. _____

2. _____

3. _____

4. _____

5. _____

Writing Nonfiction

Do you know how to do something really well? Can you teach other people how to do it? That's another genre: instructional writing or "how-to."

READ this story.

How to Fly a Paper Helicopter

What you'll need:
- Paper or cardboard
- 1 paper clip
- Scissors

It's easy to make a helicopter.

Step 1: Cut a strip of cardboard or heavy paper that's 1 inch wide and 11 inches long.

Step 2: From one end of the strip, make a cut halfway through to the middle of the strip. This part will be the wings.

Step 3: Put your scissors about a half inch below the wings and make a small cut in toward the middle from both sides. (Don't cut all the way through.) This will be the body of your helicopter.

Step 4: Fold the sides of the body in so that it's kind of skinny.

Step 5: Then fold up the end of the body and slip on a paper clip.

Step 6: Fold the wings down in two different directions, so that they split and look like the top of a *Y*.

Step 7: Time to fly! Hold your helicopter by the paper clip and throw it up as high as you can. It should come spinning down, just like a whirly-bird.

LIST five things you could teach people to do.

1. _____

2. _____

3. _____

4. _____

5. _____

Nonfiction doesn't mean boring—in fact, no writing should be boring. Sports and adventure are nonfiction genres too. And there's nothing boring about them!

READ this story.

Ship versus Ice

The *Endurance* was well named. She was a strong ship, built to withstand the crushing impact of the ice in the seas around Antarctica. Throughout the winter, she was frozen, locked in the ice that had grown until there was no more sea except deep below. Even then, *Endurance* lived up to her name. Then came spring. The air became a little warmer, the ice began to break, and the crew began to hope. Yes, the ice broke. It moved, it bucked, and it slammed. The huge ice floes were more dangerous as they wakened from their winter slumber and broke apart. *Endurance* couldn't take the punishment. Her hull splintered. The water poured in. The crew packed up their things, and carried their lifeboats with them down onto the ice floes. They could still walk for miles on the frozen, moving sea.

LIST five real-life adventures or true sports stories you'd like to write about.

1. _____

2. _____

3. _____

4. _____

5. _____

Writing Nonfiction

Since nonfiction is all about facts, you really need to know your stuff. In other words, you need to RESEARCH your topic.

There are three ways to research a topic:

1. You can go someplace and see something (like a museum).
2. You can read something (like a magazine article).
3. You can ask someone (like an expert).

FILL IN the blanks.

Topic: Snowboarding

1. Where could you go to research snowboarding?

_____

_____

_____

2. What could you read about snowboarding?

_____

_____

_____

3. Who could you ask about snowboarding?

_____

_____

_____

✓ Check It!

Cut out the Check It! section on page 1, and see if you got the answers right.
Then you'll be ready to start writing.

Bio Interview

For a biography, the best research you can do is to interview the person you want to write about.

LIST five questions you would ask someone to write their biography. Then find someone to ask, or ask yourself. FILL IN the answers.

1. Question: _____

_____

Answer: _____

_____

_____

2. Question: _____

_____

Answer: _____

_____

_____

3. Question: _____

_____

Answer: _____

_____

_____

4. Question: _____

_____

Answer: _____

_____

_____

Author! Author!

Now it's your turn. WRITE a short biography (or autobiography) based on the interview you did on the last page.

_____

_____

_____

_____

_____

_____

_____

_____

_____

_____

_____

_____

_____

_____

_____

_____

_____

You've seen how many nonfiction topics you can write about. Now it's time to make a choice. Look back over your ideas from pages 2 through 5. Pick your favorites and think of some more.

LIST five nonfiction topics that you might want to write about.

1. _____

2. _____

3. _____

4. _____

5. _____

Now, WRITE your favorite genre.

_____

✓ Check It!

Page 10

Pizza Topic Suggestions:
• How pizza came to America
• The best pizza in town
• Pizza world records
• Pizza all over the world

Dinosaur Topic Suggestions:
• Vegetarian dinosaurs
• Biggest dinosaurs
• Humans in the time of dinosaurs
• Digging up dinosaur bones
• Where dinosaurs lived

Pages 12-13

1. Famous athletes
2. New York City
3. Piano lessons
4. Aliens: fact and fiction
5. Riding a skateboard
6. Castles
7. Professional wrestlers
8. Playground games
9. Killer whales
10. Music from around the world
11. Animals of Australia
12. Crazy world records

Page 14

1. b   3. b
2. a   4. a

Pages 15-16

Suggestions:
1. When it comes to ice cream, there are way more than thirty-one flavors out there.
2. Early bedtimes for weekdays might make sense, but on the weekend, bedtimes should be much later.
3. Before you head out to the beach this summer, make sure you've got everything you need.
4. Planning a party? Here are some great ideas.
5. Everyone knows the best kind of pet is a cat. Here's why.
6. Siblings can be a total pain, but you know deep down you love them, right?
7. Don't let a little rain get you down. There's plenty of stuff to do indoors.
8. Next time you see a buzzing bee, take a closer look.
9. Some sports were meant to be played, not watched.

Wait a minute! Are any of your topics too big for a one-page story? For example, the topic of "pizza" is just too big. Let's break it down.

LIST five smaller topics that fit under the big topic of pizza.

Pizza Topics:

My favorite toppings _____

_____

_____

_____

_____

Try it again, this time with dinosaurs.

Dinosaur Topics:

Tyrannosaurus Rex _____

_____

_____

_____

_____

Now, GO BACK to your topic list on page 9. PICK two of your topics and break them into smaller topics.

Big Topic:

_____

Small Topic:

_____

_____

_____

_____

Big Topic:

_____

Small Topic:

_____

_____

_____

_____

Don't forget about research. Pick a topic that you know a lot about, or that you want to learn more about.

Which of these topics do you know the most about?

_____

Which of these topics would you like to learn more about?

_____

So, which topic do you most want to write about?

_____

Congratulations—you've picked a topic!

Topic & Topic Sentence

Your readers need to know your topic right away. They get it from your TOPIC SENTENCE. That's usually the first sentence (or two) of your story.

READ each topic sentence. Then, FILL IN the blanks with the right topics from the box.

Topics

Animals of Australia	Famous athletes	Aliens: fact and fiction
Crazy world records	Music from around the world	Professional wrestlers
Castles		Piano lessons
New York City	Playground games	
Riding a skateboard	Killer whales	

1. **Topic:** _____

   Sentence: Some sports stars are known all over the world.

2. **Topic:** _____

   Sentence: The Big Apple. Gotham City. The largest city in the United States goes by many names.

3. **Topic:** _____

   Sentence: If you think learning to play scales is a waste of time, think again.

4. **Topic:** _____

   Sentence: When it comes to life in outer space, it's important to separate the truth from the tall tales.

5. **Topic:** _____

   Sentence: There's no better way to cruise down the sidewalk than on four wheels and a board.

6. **Topic:** _____

   Sentence: Kings and queens sure know how to live large, in houses fit for royalty.

7. **Topic:** _____

   Sentence: Behind their masks and wild behavior, most professional wrestlers are real athletes.

8. **Topic:** _____

   Sentence: From kickball to four square, some of the best games come from the playground.

9. **Topic:** _____

   Sentence: The first thing you need to know about killer whales is that they're actually dolphins.

10. **Topic:** _____

    Sentence: People from every nation groove to their own special beat.

11. **Topic:** _____

    Sentence: From kangaroos to quokkas, Australia is home to many interesting animals.

12. **Topic:** _____

    Sentence: Some people will do anything to set a world record.

A good topic sentence doesn't just say what the story is about. It grabs the reader's attention. Don't be a boring writer. A bored reader usually stops reading.

READ the topic sentences below. CHECK the ones that are *not* boring.

1. **Topic: Hershey's Chocolate**

   ☐ a. The Hershey Chocolate Company was started in 1894 in Derry Church, PA (now called Hershey, PA).

   ☐ b. Hershey bars are so big they named a town after them.

2. **Topic: Charlie Chaplin**

   ☐ a. Charlie Chaplin packed a lot of living into his 77 years.

   ☐ b. Charlie Chaplin lived to be 77 years old. He made more than 90 movies, won three Academy Awards, wrote hundreds of songs, and was married three times.

3. **Topic: Prairie Dogs**

   ☐ a. Prairie dogs are a type of squirrel and bark when they sense danger.

   ☐ b. What do you call a squirrel that barks? A prairie dog, that's what!

4. **Topic: The History of Basketball**

   ☐ a. Believe it or not, the first basketball game was played with a soccer ball and a peach basket.

   ☐ b. The game of basketball was invented in 1891. The first players used a peach basket for a hoop and a soccer ball.

Now it's your turn. WRITE a topic sentence (or two) for each of these topics.

HINT: Don't worry if you only know a little about the topic.

1. **Topic: Ice cream flavors**

   _____

   _____

2. **Topic: Weekend bedtimes**

   _____

   _____

3. **Topic: Things to bring when you go to the beach**

   _____

   _____

4. **Topic: Great party ideas**

   _____

   _____

5. **Topic: The best kind of pets**

   _____

   _____

6. **Topic: Brothers and sisters**

_____

_____

7. **Topic: Things to do on a rainy day**

_____

_____

8. **Topic: Bees**

_____

_____

9. **Topic: Sports that are boring to watch on TV**

_____

_____

Finally, WRITE the topic sentence for the topic you picked on page 11.

_____

_____

✓ Check It!

Cut out the Check It! section on page 9, and see if you got the answers right.

Now that you have a topic and a topic sentence, how do you fill the rest of the page? Easy! Just use MAIN IDEAS and DETAILS. You'll need to MAP them out before you write. FILL IN the blanks with supporting details from the box.

Topic: Birds

Details

parakeets	worms	songbirds	birds of prey
cockatoos	waterbirds	small animals	
fruit	budgerigars	seeds	

Main Ideas

Types of Birds

1. _____
2. _____
3. _____

Bird Food

1. _____
2. _____
3. _____
4. _____

Bird Pets

1. _____
2. _____
3. _____

When you map out your story, you start with your main ideas, and you support them with details.

✓ **Check It!**

Page 17

Types of Birds: water birds, songbirds, birds of prey
Bird Food: worms, seeds, small animals, fruit
Bird Pets: parakeets, cockatoos, budgerigars

Pages 18-19

Main Idea 1: What's a snail?
Supporting Details:
1. Snails are mollusks.
2. Mollusks are animals with no bones.
3. A snail without a shell is called a *slug*.

Main Idea 2: Snail description
Supporting Details:
1. Snails are about 1.5 inches long.
2. Some snails have spiral-shaped shells.
3. Some snails have eyes on the end of tentacles.

Main Idea 3: How snails move
Supporting Details:
1. Snails glide along using one muscular foot.
2. They only go about 1 mm per second.
3. They use mucus to slide and avoid injury.

Main Idea 4: Snails and food
Supporting Details:
1. Snails eat fruits and vegetables.
2. People eat snails.
3. In France, a dish of snails is called *escargot*.

Mapping

Before you write a nonfiction story, you should MAP it.

FILL IN the nonfiction story map on the next page with the main ideas and details in the list.

Topic: Snails

Some have spiral-shaped shells.

Snails and food

Mollusks are animals with no bones.

In France, a dish of snails is called *escargot*.

Some snails have eyes on the end of tentacles.

What's a snail?

Snails glide along using one muscular foot.

A snail is a mollusk.

A snail without a shell is called a *slug*.

Snail description

Snails are about 1.5 inches long.

Snails use mucus to slide and avoid injury while moving.

People eat snails.

How snails move

Snails eat mostly fruits and vegetables.

Snails travel at speeds of about 1 millimeter per second.

Page 20

Details suggestions:
Hamburgers
French fries
Fried chicken
McDonald's
Wendy's
Burger King
High fat content
High sugar content in soda
High salt content
Drive-through windows
Premade food
Quick ordering process

Main Ideas suggestions:
Fast food restaurants
Kinds of fast food
Fast food is bad for you.
Fast food is FAST.

Topic Sentence Suggestion:
Americans like their food, and they like it FAST.

Page 21

Suggestions:
Topic sentence: Americans like their food, and they like it FAST!

Main Idea 1: Kinds of fast food
Supporting Details:
1. Hamburgers
2. French fries
3. Fried chicken

Main Idea 2: Fast food restaurants
Supporting Details:
1. McDonald's
2. Wendy's
3. Burger King

Main Idea 3: Fast food is FAST.
Supporting Details:
1. Premade food
2. Quick ordering process
3. Drive-through windows

Main Idea 4: Fast food is bad for you.
Supporting Details:
1. High fat content
2. High salt content
3. High sugar content in sodas

Topic: Snails

Topic Sentence
Believe it or not, a snail
is an animal, not a bug.

Paragraph 1. Main Idea

_____

_____

Supporting Details

1. _____

2. _____

3. _____

Paragraph 2. Main Idea

_____

_____

Supporting Details

1. _____

2. _____

3. _____

Paragraph 3. Main Idea

_____

_____

Supporting Details

1. _____

2. _____

3. _____

Paragraph 4. Main Idea

_____

_____

Supporting Details

1. _____

2. _____

3. _____

To make your own map, start by writing down everything you know about a topic.

HINT: You don't need to write full sentences.

Topic: Fast Food

WRITE DOWN everything you know about fast food.

_____

_____

_____

_____

_____

_____

_____

_____

_____

_____

Read over your list. Is it mostly details? Can you fit them together?

LIST your main ideas.

_____

_____

Also, WRITE a topic sentence for this topic.

_____

Now, FILL IN this nonfiction story map with the information you wrote down on the previous page.

HINT: Use as many of the boxes as you need. Feel free to add more on a separate piece of paper.

Topic: Fast Food
Topic Sentence

_____

Paragraph 1. Main Idea

_____

Supporting Details

1. _____

2. _____

3. _____

Paragraph 2. Main Idea

_____

Supporting Details

1. _____

2. _____

3. _____

Paragraph 3. Main Idea

_____

Supporting Details

1. _____

2. _____

3. _____

Paragraph 4. Main Idea

_____

Supporting Details

1. _____

2. _____

3. _____

✔ **Check It!**

Cut out the Check It! section on page 17, and see if you got the answers right.

Mapping

Now it's time to map out the topic you picked on page 11.

Topic: _____

WRITE DOWN everything you know about your topic.

_____

_____

_____

_____

_____

_____

_____

_____

_____

_____

_____

_____

_____

_____

_____

_____

_____

_____

Are you having trouble with your facts? Don't forget to RESEARCH if you need to check the facts or learn some more.

WRITE some questions you still have about your topic.

_____

_____

_____

_____

Where can you GO to answer these questions?

_____

_____

_____

_____

What can you READ to answer these questions?

_____

_____

_____

_____

Who can you ASK to answer these questions?

_____

_____

_____

_____

Now, TURN the page to fill in your map.

Mapping

Now, FILL IN this nonfiction story map with the information you wrote down on the previous page. Don't forget your topic sentence from page 16.

Topic:

Topic Sentence:

_____

_____

Paragraph 1. Main Idea

_____

_____

Supporting Details

1. _____

2. _____

3. _____

Paragraph 2. Main Idea

_____

_____

Supporting Details

1. _____

2. _____

3. _____

Paragraph 3. Main Idea

_____

_____

Supporting Details

1. _____

2. _____

3. _____

Paragraph 4. Main Idea

_____

_____

Supporting Details

1. _____

2. _____

3. _____

Writing an Argument

4

Some nonfiction topics give you the chance to express your opinion. When you use facts to support your opinions, you're making an ARGUMENT. A good writer makes strong arguments.

READ this argument story.

> **It Just Doesn't Make Cents.**
>
> Pennies are a waste of money. That's right! It costs almost *two* cents to make one new penny. Pennies aren't even useful. They don't work in gumball machines or arcade games or anything else. Yet every year, we keep making more. You see, the state of Illinois puts up a fight any time somebody tries to make pennies go away. Why? Because President Abraham Lincoln was born in Illinois. (Remember whose face is on the penny?) It simply doesn't make sense to keep making cents. Join the fight!

1. CHECK the author's opinion about pennies.

    ☐ a. The author thinks pennies are useful.

    ☐ b. The author thinks pennies are a waste of money.

LIST the facts that the author uses to support this opinion.

2. _____

3. _____

4. _____

Ta-da! Facts turn an opinion into an argument.

✓ Check It!

Page 25

1. b
2. It costs more than a penny to make a penny.
3. You can't use pennies in vending machines.
4. Illinois only defends the penny because Abe Lincoln is on it.

Page 26

Suggestions:

Topic: Testing drugs on animals
Testing drugs on animals is wrong because most animal testing labs treat animals badly, and the animals usually die.

Topic: Tearing down the rain forest
Tearing down rain forests is wrong because it can destroy the habitats of entire species, which can lead to extinction.

Topic: People who paint grafitti on walls
People who paint grafitti on walls should be punished severely because they harm other people's property.

Page 27

1. Vote for Benny Howell for karate club president.
2. Give money to the Fund for Polar Bears.

When you're writing an argument, your topic sentence is your opinion. (Look back at the penny story as an example.) It's really important that your readers know right away that you're writing an argument.

FILL IN the blanks to make some quick arguments.

Topic: Kids getting to vote

What's your opinion? Kids should get to vote.

Why? Because the government makes laws that affect kids.

Don't forget to fill in the "Why?" with a fact. That's what makes it an argument.

Topic: Testing drugs on animals

What's your opinion? _____

_____

Why? _____

Topic: Tearing down the rain forest

What's your opinion? _____

_____

Why? _____

Topic: People who paint grafitti on walls

What's your opinion? _____

_____

Why? _____

Those are some good arguments because each one is backed up with facts.

Sometimes you write an argument because you're trying to get your readers to do something. That's when you end your argument with a CALL TO ACTION.

READ these stories. They're missing their calls to action.

Time to Vote

Benny Howell would be a great karate club president. First of all, Benny's been in the club longer than anybody else. Plus, out of all the kids in the club, he ranks the highest in karate skills. Finally, Benny has promised that if he's elected president, he will try to get the karate school to add more classes on Saturdays.

What does the author want you to do?

WRITE the call to action. _____

_____

Polar Bears Need YOU!

The Fund for Polar Bears is a really worthy cause. Polar bears don't have as many safe places to float while they search for food because the Arctic ice is shrinking. There are experts who study the ways that global warming affects polar bears. Their research could save the bears, but research costs money and they don't have much of that.

WRITE the call to action. _____

_____

Writing an Argument

Here's your chance to map some important arguments.

FILL IN the blanks.

Topic: Your bedtime

Opinion: _____

_____

Facts: _____

_____

_____

_____

_____

Call to action: _____

_____

Topic: Your allowance

Opinion: _____

_____

Facts: _____

_____

_____

_____

_____

Call to action: _____

_____

Topic: Having a pet

Opinion: _____

_____

Facts: _____

_____

_____

_____

_____

Call to action: _____

_____

TURN the page to WRITE your arguments.

HINTS:

1. START with your opinion as the topic sentence.

2. SUPPORT your opinion with facts from the fact list.

3. END by stating your goal and call to action.

Author! Author!

WRITE the argument about your bedtime, using the map on page 28.

_____

_____

_____

_____

_____

_____

_____

_____

_____

_____

_____

_____

_____

_____

_____

_____

_____

Author! Author!

WRITE the argument about your allowance, using the map on page 28.

_____

_____

_____

_____

_____

_____

_____

_____

_____

_____

_____

_____

_____

_____

_____

_____

_____

_____

_____

Author! Author!

WRITE the argument about having a pet, using the map on page 29.

_____

_____

_____

_____

_____

_____

_____

_____

_____

_____

_____

_____

_____

_____

_____

_____

_____

_____

_____

_____

_____

A DRAFT is your first try at writing a story. It's for your eyes only. DRAFTING is when you write a story over and over until you get it right.

First, READ this story map and FILL IN the blanks.

Topic:

Topic Sentence

_____

_____

Main Idea 1: Indoor Fun

1. Video games _____

2. Board games _____

3. _____

Main Idea 2: Outdoor Fun

1. Skateboarding _____

2. Bike riding _____

3. _____

Now let's turn this map into a story.

✓ **Check It!**

Page 33

Suggestions:
Topic: Fun
Topic Sentence: You can have fun inside and out.
Main Idea 1: Indoor Fun
Details:
1. Video games
2. Board games
3. Watching TV
Main Idea 2: Outdoor Fun
Details:
1. Skateboarding
2. Bike riding
3. Playing with a pet

Page 34

Suggestions:
Main Idea 1: There are lots of ways to have fun outside.
Details:
1. You can play video or computer games.
2. You can play board games like checkers.
3. You can watch your favorite TV shows.
Main Idea 2: There are also tons of fun things you can do outside.
Details:
1. Skateboarding, for example, is super fun.
2. There's nothing more fun than riding a bike.
3. If you have a pet, you can play together outside.

Page 35

Suggestion:
You can have fun indoors and out. There are lots of ways to have fun inside the house. You can play video or computer games, for one thing. How about playing a board game like checkers? Of course, you can always watch TV.

Page 36

Suggestion:
If you'd rather have fun in the sun, there's plenty to do outside too. Skateboarding and bike riding, for example, are super fun. If you have a pet, you and Fido can go outside and run around.

No matter where you are, you can find something fun to do if you just look around.

Drafting

Let's start by turning our main ideas and details into complete sentences.

HINT: A complete sentence has a subject, a verb, and an object.
Example: The *subject* kicked the *object*. (*Kicked* is the verb.)

REWRITE the details from the story map to make them complete sentences.

Main Idea 1: There are lots of ways to have fun outside.

1. You can play video or computer games.

2. _____

_____

3. _____

_____

Main Idea 2: _____

1. _____

_____

2. _____

_____

3. _____

_____

A good story always uses complete sentences.

Now that you've got your sentences, you need to put them together to make paragraphs.

First, REREAD your sentences on the previous page. Then ANSWER these questions.

1. Do all your sentences start with the same words?   CIRCLE one: YES   NO
   Each sentence should start a different way.

2. Does every detail need its own sentence?   CIRCLE one: YES   NO
   It's okay to combine some of your details into the same sentence.

WRITE the first paragraph of this story.

HINT: Start with the topic sentence and then Main Idea 1.

_____

_____

_____

_____

_____

_____

_____

_____

_____

_____

_____

_____

_____

_____

_____

_____

_____

Drafting

For the second paragraph, you'll need to start with a TRANSITION. A transition is a way to tell your readers that you're moving to a new main idea. Transitions work between sentences inside a paragraph too. Some transitions are listed in the box.

On the other hand	For example	Of course	However
First of all	Second of all	Next	Then
Finally	Also		

WRITE your second paragraph.

_____

_____

_____

_____

_____

_____

Now we need a CONCLUSION—an ending. It's like the topic sentence, only it's written differently. (If you're writing an argument, the conclusion might be your call to action.)

WRITE your conclusion.

_____

_____

_____

_____

_____

_____

You did it! You wrote a draft.

Let's write another draft. FILL IN this nonfiction story map.

Topic: The People in My Life

Topic Sentence

_____

_____

Main Idea: My Family

_____

_____

_____

_____

_____

_____

_____

_____

_____

Main Idea: My Friends

_____

_____

_____

_____

_____

_____

_____

_____

_____

TURN the page to write your draft.

HINTS:
1. Write the details into sentences.
2. Combine the sentences into main idea paragraphs.
3. Make the paragraphs flow into each other by using transitions.
4. End with your conclusion.

Author! Author!

WRITE a story draft, using the nonfiction story map on the previous page.

_____

_____

_____

_____

_____

_____

_____

_____

_____

_____

_____

_____

_____

_____

_____

_____

_____

_____

_____

_____

_____

_____

Author! Author!

It's showtime! Using your nonfiction story map from page 24, WRITE a draft of your story.

_____

_____

_____

_____

_____

_____

_____

_____

_____

_____

_____

_____

_____

_____

_____

_____

_____

_____

_____

_____

_____

_____

TURN the page for more space to write.

Drafting

When you make up a story, that's FICTION. You can get your ideas from real life or from your amazing imagination.

Fiction has GENRES like the nonfiction genres we learned about in the first lesson. Do you know any fiction genres?

WRITE DOWN all the kinds of stories you can think of.

Fantasy _____

_____

_____

_____

_____

_____

_____

What's your favorite genre of story to read?

_____

✓ Check It!

Page 41

Suggestions:
Action/Adventure
Contemporary
Historical
Horror
Humor
Romance
Science fiction
Western

Page 46

1. NOT original
2. Original
3. NOT original
4. Original
5. Original
6. NOT original
7. NOT original
8. Original
9. NOT original
10. Original

Writing Fiction

READ this FANTASY story.

> **Fairy War**
>
> As the day of the battle drew nearer, each side brought on more fighters. The fairies of the north had the bears and the elk. The mighty horns of the moose could do a lot of damage. The fairies of the south asked for help from the leopards and the pythons. These stealthy warriors would hide in the trees and drop down to kill their opponents.
>
> The entire world knew that no matter which side won, this battle was going to be the bloodiest anyone had ever seen.

If there's magic, animals talking, or anything that couldn't happen in the real world, then it's a FANTASY.

LIST fantasy stories that you've read.

Harry Potter & The Sorcerer's Stone by J.K. Rowling

_____

_____

_____

_____

_____

_____

_____

_____

READ this HISTORICAL story.

Streetcar Sally

Sally Singleton rode the Chicago streetcars all day. She liked the streetcars better than the new elevated trains because it was easier to watch the people hurrying down the streets from the streetcar. Sally figured the city had to move fast since all the stores and factories and houses needed to be rebuilt after the Great Fire.

Every day, Sally made one stop. She got off on Michigan Avenue, right near the Loop, and stepped inside her favorite candy shop. Dozens of giant glass jars filled the shelves behind the counter. Sally would hand her penny to Mr. Strubel, the owner, and point to a jar. Sometimes she picked licorice strings. Other days she wanted candy hearts. But every time, just as Mr. Strubel was about to scoop out her candy, she would say, "No, Mr. Strubel. Not from the top! I want the candy on the bottom."

Mr. Strubel always groaned when he saw Streetcar Sally come into his shop.

If a story is set in the past, then it's HISTORICAL fiction.

LIST historical stories that you've read.

The Witch of Blackbird Pond by Elizabeth George Speare

READ this HORROR story.

Ghoul School

Alex knew that Ravenwood Elementary was weird the minute he walked through the doors. The halls were so quiet. All the kids just shuffled to their classrooms in silence.

The teachers were even stranger. Alex couldn't tell if they were walking or floating. They moaned in an eerie, echoey way. When they walked by, Alex's hair stood on end and he felt an ice-cold chill. Once he saw a teacher go directly *through* a student!

Alex's mom and dad didn't believe his story, so he waited until the first parent-teacher conference. That night, he tried to warn them one last time. They laughed.

And they never came back.

If a story tries to give you the creeps, then it's a HORROR story.

LIST horror stories that you've read.

The Goosebumps series by R. L. Stine

_____

_____

_____

_____

_____

_____

_____

_____

_____

Many great stories don't seem to have a genre at all. They're called CONTEMPORARY because they're set in the present day—no magic, no aliens, no ghosts.

READ this CONTEMPORARY story.

Earl Does It Again

At Hiawatha Summer Camp, the campers knew one thing for sure. They knew that every Friday Earl would get away and find a way into town. He always found a new way to escape. Once he hid in a hamper filled with dirty sheets going to the laundromat. Another time, he snuck into the backseat of the cook's car as he drove into town for supplies. As soon as Earl got there, he would see a movie, ride his skateboard, and buy a boatload of candy to share with his cabin.

When it got close to dinnertime, Earl would go to see Mrs. Beecher at the post office and use her phone to call the camp. He'd be back in his cabin twenty minutes later.

One day, someone asked him why he bothered coming back at all.

"I have to come back," he said. "Friday is cookout night. I love barbecue!"

LIST contemporary stories that you've read.

Because of Winn-Dixie by Kate DiCamillo

Your story ideas, especially your characters, need to be ORIGINAL. If your idea uses the same names and places that you've seen on TV or read in another book, then they're not original.

CHECK the original ideas in the list.

1. ☐ A sponge named Bob wears square pants and has undersea adventures.

2. ☐ A mouse wants to be an astronaut, so he sneaks onto the space shuttle.

3. ☐ A red monster named Elmo lives on Sesame Street.

4. ☐ Two knights of the Round Table go on a quest to save a princess.

5. ☐ A kid steals a pack of gum from the store and gets caught.

6. ☐ A toy named Buzz Lightyear teams up with his friend Woody for an adventure.

7. ☐ A girl named Dora becomes an explorer with her friend Boots the monkey.

8. ☐ A city of rabbits has to fight off a giant cat.

9. ☐ A kid named Harry Potter finds out he's a wizard.

10. ☐ Five goats form a rock band and travel the world.

Some ideas, like the story of *Little Red Riding Hood*, are so old that it's okay to rewrite them. Stories like that have been around for hundreds of years and have been retold a million times. If you use them, you should always add your own special twist.

You can NEVER copy words directly out of a book for your stories. Never.

Coming up with ideas can be the hardest part about writing.

LIST five ideas for contemporary stories. Remember: no magic, no ghosts, no aliens.

1. _____

2. _____

3. _____

4. _____

5. _____

Now LIST five ideas for fantasy stories.

1. _____

2. _____

3. _____

4. _____

5. _____

Writing Fiction

Keep coming up with ideas.

LIST five ideas for horror stories. Make them spine-tingling!

1. _____

2. _____

3. _____

4. _____

5. _____

LIST five ideas for historical stories. Think about which time periods you'd like to write about.

1. _____

2. _____

3. _____

4. _____

5. _____

Most good fiction stories have characters that struggle with a problem. Let's take *The Three Little Pigs* as our example.

✓ Check It!

Page 49

Suggestions:
Characters: Larry, Curly, Squiggles, and the Big Bad Wolf
Setting: Piggieville, a suburb of Hogtown
Problem: The wolf keeps blowing the pigs' houses down.
Solution: The pigs hide in a house made of bricks and pour hot oil on the wolf.

Who are the characters in *The Three Little Pigs*?
HINT: You can name the characters anything you like.

_____

_____

_____

Where do the three pigs live?
HINT: You can make this up too.

_____

_____

_____

What's the problem in *The Three Little Pigs*?

_____

_____

_____

How do the three pigs solve this problem?

_____

_____

_____

You did it! You just mapped a story.

Stories are always about CHARACTERS. They don't have to be humans, but they usually act like humans. Good characters want something, like to be treated like a grownup or win the big game.

FILL IN the blanks to make some great characters.

1. <u>Billy</u> is a <u>boy</u>
   NAME   TYPE

   who <u>wants to ride a bike</u>.
        WANTS

2. _____ is a <u>carrot</u>
   NAME   TYPE

   who _____.
        WANTS

3. <u>Minerva</u> is a _____
   NAME   TYPE

   who <u>wants to rule the world</u>.
        WANTS

4. _____ is a _____
   NAME   TYPE

   who <u>wants to make a friend</u>.
        WANTS

5. _____ is a <u>hamster</u>
   NAME   TYPE

   who _____.
        WANTS

Now you need a place for your characters to hang out. That's called the SETTING. You can make up settings just like you make up characters.

FILL IN the blanks to create fun settings.

1. <u>Tunnelvania</u> is a <u>city</u> that's
   NAME   TYPE

   <u>completely underground</u>.
   DESCRIPTION

2. <u> </u> is a <u>street</u> that's
   NAME   TYPE

   <u> </u>.
   DESCRIPTION

3. <u>Hog Hollow</u> is a <u> </u> that's
   NAME   TYPE

   <u>where all the pigs live</u>.
   DESCRIPTION

4. <u> </u> is a <u> </u> that's
   NAME   TYPE

   <u>floating in the sky</u>.
   DESCRIPTION

5. <u> </u> is a <u>building</u> that's
   NAME   TYPE

   <u> </u>.
   DESCRIPTION

Now your characters have an amazing world to explore!

Mapping

When you write a story, you have to give your characters big PROBLEMS. The best way to make trouble for characters is to make it hard for them to get what they want.

GO BACK to page 50 and make up a story problem for each of the characters. LIST the problems.

Story Problems

Billy can't have a bike because his family is poor. _____

_____

_____

_____

_____

_____

_____

_____

_____

_____

_____

Phew! That's a lot of problems. Do you feel bad for your characters?

Now comes the good part: You get to solve your characters' problems.

GO BACK to the previous page and make up SOLUTIONS for all of those problems. WRITE the solutions.

Story Solutions

Billy gets a part-time job to save money to buy a bike.

_____

_____

_____

_____

_____

_____

_____

_____

_____

_____

_____

Isn't it fun to make your characters happy in the end?

Fiction Story Map

FINISH the story map, using your fabulous imagination.

Main Character(s)

Renny, a fly who likes

to drink soda

_____

_____

_____

Problem	**Title**	**Solution**
_____		_____
_____		_____
_____	_____	_____
_____		_____

Setting

_____

_____

_____

_____

_____

Fiction Story Map

FINISH the story map.

Main Character(s)

_____

_____

_____

_____

_____

Problem

_____

_____

_____

_____

_____

Title

_____

Solution

_____

_____

_____

_____

Setting

Blub-Blub,

a city beneath the sea

_____

_____

_____

Fiction Story Map

Use your own great ideas for this story map.

The genre of my story is _____ .

Main Character(s)
_____
_____
_____
_____
_____

Problem	Title	Solution
_____		_____
_____		_____
_____	_____	_____
_____		_____
_____		_____

Setting
_____
_____
_____
_____
_____

PLOT is what happens in a fiction story. You need action and suspense to keep your readers reading.

Let's go back to the *The Three Little Pigs*.

What happens first?

<u>First, the pigs each build a house: one of straw, one of sticks,</u>

<u>one of bricks.</u>

What happens next?

_____

_____

Then what happens?

_____

_____

Then what happens?

_____

_____

What do the pigs want?

_____

_____

How many times do the pigs try to get what they want?

_____

Lots of good stories are built like *The Three Little Pigs*.

✓ Check It!

Page 57

First, the pigs each build a house: one of straw, one of sticks, one of bricks.
   Then, the wolf blows down the straw house.
   Next, the wolf blows down the stick house.
   Then, the wolf tries to blow down the brick house, but he can't.
   The pigs want to be safe from the wolf.
   They try three times to get what they want.

Page 58

Suggestions:
   Stinky puts on perfume.
   She rolls around in mud to cover the smell.
   She eats a lot of flowers.

Page 59

Suggestions:
   Stinky puts on perfume, but the perfume made her smell worse.
B
   Finally, she tries covering up the smell with mud. The mud works, but she hates being so dirty. She decides she'd rather just be stinky.

Page 60

Suggestions:
   Hamlet is loud. Merv is quiet.
   First, Hamlet shows how he is louder than Merv.
   Merv's so quiet the audience has to sit still to hear him.
   Next, Hamlet wears a bright costume so everyone can see him.
   Merv uses his sad face to make everyone cry.
   Finally, Hamlet gives up and leaves the theater.
   Merv tries to do Hamlet's show, but he can't do comedy. Hamlet realizes he's funny and Merv is the serious actor. They become best friends.

 **Check It!**

Page 61

Suggestions:

The girls in Janine's new town have have rolled-up jeans and green shoelaces in their shoes. Janine has wide-legged jeans and white shoelaces.

First, Janine puts green shoelaces in her shoes.

The next day, all the girls have white shoelaces.

Janine buys jeans and wears them rolled up.

The next day, the girls are wearing wide-legged jeans.

Finally, Janine wears all her old clothes. All the girls now fit in with Janine.

It works! She doesn't need to change.

Just like the three pigs, your main character should want something very badly. The plot of your story is what happens when he tries to get what he wants.

Take this character, for example:
Stinky, a skunk who wants to smell pretty

What can Stinky do to get what she wants? LIST things she can try.

<u>She tries to take a bubble bath.</u>

_____

_____

_____

_____

_____

_____

_____

_____

_____

_____

That's a lot of trying! CIRCLE your three favorites.

A story is boring if the main character gets what he wants right away. Some kind of obstacle has to make it hard. That's the story problem. It has to be so hard to solve that the character actually fails the first couple of times he tries.

Let's go back to Stinky the skunk. Do any of her solutions work?

FILL IN the blanks for why Stinky can't lose her smell. (Use what you circled on the previous page.)

What does Stinky try first?

She tries to take a bubble bath.

Why doesn't it work?

A few minutes after the bath, her smell comes back.

What does Stinky try next?

_____

Why doesn't it work?

_____

Now you've got two choices:
 A. Stinky could destink herself.
 B. Stinky could fail, but she learns to like herself the way she is, stink and all.

Which do you choose? CIRCLE one: A   B

Okay, based on your choice, FILL IN Stinky's final try.

What does Stinky try last?

_____

What happens?

_____

Plot

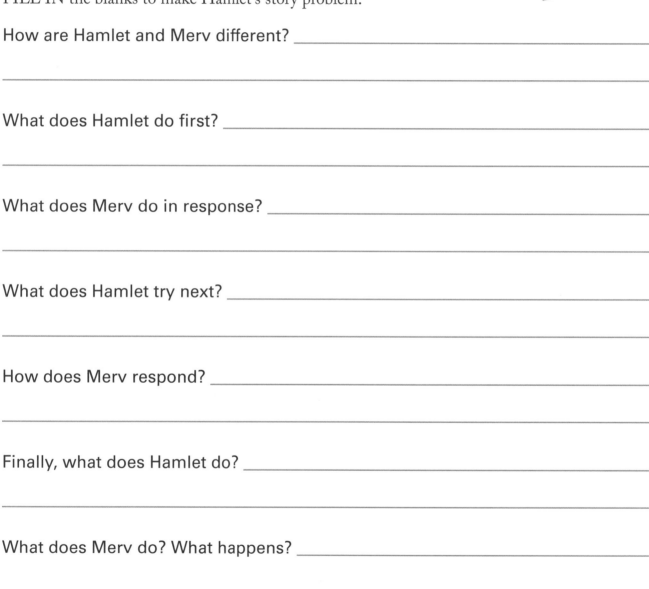

Another way to get your story problem started is to bring in a new character, someone who doesn't want your main character to get what he wants.

Here are two new characters for us to work with:

1. *Hamlet, a man who wants to be the best actor in his town*
2. *A guy named Merv who moves to Hamlet's town, claiming to be the best actor*

FILL IN the blanks to make Hamlet's story problem.

How are Hamlet and Merv different? _____

_____

What does Hamlet do first? _____

_____

What does Merv do in response? _____

_____

What does Hamlet try next? _____

_____

How does Merv respond? _____

_____

Finally, what does Hamlet do? _____

_____

What does Merv do? What happens? _____

_____

Each time a character tries to get what he wants and fails, he should try harder the next time, wanting it even more. That way, your readers will get more and more excited.

Another way to cause trouble for your characters is to put them in a new situation, around people and places they don't know (and maybe don't like).

Here's our character:
Janine, a teenager who just moved to a new town and wants to fit in

FILL IN the blanks to make Janine's story problem.

Why does Janine think she doesn't fit in? _____

_____

What does she do to fit in first? _____

_____

How do people react? _____

_____

What does Janine try next? _____

_____

What happens? _____

_____

Finally, Janine makes one last try. What does she do? _____

_____

Does it work? What happens? _____

_____

Did you let Janine get what she wanted? You don't *have* to, but if your readers like your character, they probably want her to have a happy ending.

Plot

Now, FILL IN this story map, using either Hamlet or Janine's story.

Title _____

The first thing that happens is _____

_____

The problem _____

_____

After that _____

_____

After that _____

_____

The solution _____

_____

_____

Now use the character you chose for your story map on page 56.

_____ is a _____
NAME   TYPE

who _____.
WANTS

Now, LIST all the different ways your character could try to get what he or she wants.

_____

_____

_____

_____

CIRCLE your three favorites.
What's the problem? What's keeping your character from winning?

_____

_____

_____

_____

How do you want the story to end?

_____

_____

_____

_____

Now you're ready to fill in your plot map for this story.

FILL IN this plot map for the story you mapped on page 56.

Title _____

The first thing that happens is _____

_____

The problem _____

_____

After that _____

_____

After that _____

_____

The solution _____

_____

_____

Description & Dialogue

9

Stories are more than just plot and action. A story also has lots of description and dialogue.

A good DESCRIPTION uses all five senses. READ this description.

Sunday Dinner

Uncle Buck has a voice like a cow mooing. He bellows his questions, like, "So, Danny, how's schooooool?" Add this to the sound of plates and forks and talk, and you can tell how loud Sunday dinner can be at my house.

On Sundays, the house smells like meat and fried potatoes all day, a smell that sticks to your clothes and hair. Mom turns on the chandelier over the table, and little beams of light shoot all over the room, shining off the dishes and silverware. The Sunday cloth napkins slip off our laps and rub like burlap over our mouths when we wipe our faces.

Dad's roast beef is worth it though. It's not chewy but soft and salty and full of beefy flavor that matches the smell in the air but is ten times better. We wash it down with thick, buttery milk from the farm down the road. I wish Sunday came twice a week!

WRITE the parts of the description that fit each sense.

Smell _____

Sound _____

Sight _____

Taste _____

Touch _____

✓ **Check It!**

Page 65

Smell: meat and fried potatoes
Sound: Uncle Buck's voice, plates and forks and talk
Sight: the light from the chandelier
Taste: Dad's roast beef
Touch: the cloth napkins

Page 66

Suggestions:
Topic: Attics
Smell: dust, moldy clothes, tingling nose wanting to sneeze
Sound: quiet, mice rustling, clunk of a trunk opening
Sight: light coming up through holes in the floor, shadows in the corner, big trunks and boxes
Taste: dry air, cheesy mold, blood from a cut on the finger
Touch: dusty boxes, sharp trunk latch (cuts finger), rough insulation on the ceiling

Page 67

Suggestions:
Topic: Grandma
Smell: heavy perfume, face powder, laundry detergent
Sound: loud nasal voice, jangling jewelry, clicking teeth
Sight: heavy makeup, poofy hair, pointy nails, bright red hair
Taste: perfumey cheek, yummy chicken dinner
Touch: soft skin, bony hand, heavy bracelet

Page 69

1. Terry
2. Pat
3. swimming
4. They're brother and sister.

Description & Dialogue

When you're getting ready to describe an important object or place, take a minute to think about all the ways it can affect your five senses.

FILL IN this sense map about attics.

Topic: Attics

FILL IN this sense map about Grandma.

HINT: This is about a grandmother you make up, not your real granny.

Topic: Grandma

Description & Dialogue

GO BACK to the story you mapped on page 56. PICK a person, object, or place from that story.

FILL IN this sense map about your choice.

Topic: _____

_____
_____
_____

_____
_____
_____

_____
_____
_____

_____
_____
_____
_____

_____
_____
_____

Description & Dialogue

When characters talk to each other in a story, that's called DIALOGUE. You can use dialogue to show what characters are like.

READ this dialogue.

"Yo, what's the hold up?" yelled Pat. "The water's great!"

"I'm coming. The top of my suit's stuck," answered Terry. "Here I am. Oooh, it's cold."

"C'mon, jump in already!"

"Oh no!" cried Terry. "I need to use the stairs."

"Baby!" Pat snorted. "Maybe when you're big like me, you'll be braver."

"I'm not scared."

"Yes, you are."

"I'm telling Mom!"

"Go ahead."

"MOM!"

FILL IN the blanks with information you learned from the dialogue.

1. One of these characters is a girl. Which one is it?

_____

2. Which character do you think is older?

_____

3. What are these kids doing?

_____

4. How are they related?

_____

Think about it. How did you know the answers to all those questions?

Author! Author!

WRITE a conversation between a kid and a grownup talking about extreme sports.

HINT: How would they speak differently? Would they use the same kind of words? Would the grownup know as much as the kid?

_____

_____

_____

_____

_____

_____

_____

_____

_____

_____

_____

_____

_____

_____

_____

Author! Author!

WRITE a conversation between two kids sneaking into the kitchen for a midnight snack. Use only dialogue. Let the situation come out through the dialogue.

HINT: What are the kids talking about? Do they have trouble seeing in the dark? What other ways will their situation make them say certain things?

_____

_____

_____

_____

_____

_____

_____

_____

_____

_____

_____

_____

_____

_____

_____

_____

Author! Author!

GO BACK to the story you mapped on page 56. WRITE a dialogue between your main character and somebody else. MIX in some description to show where this conversation is happening. Don't forget to use all five senses.

_____

_____

_____

_____

_____

_____

_____

_____

_____

_____

_____

_____

_____

_____

_____

_____

_____

_____

It's time to write your story draft. You should start by introducing your main character.

Here's one to start with:

Main Character: Percy, a boy who wants to learn to skateboard

FILL IN the blanks.

1. How old is Percy? _____

2. What does Percy look like? _____

_____

_____

3. Where does Percy live? _____

_____

_____

4. Why does Percy want to learn to skateboard? _____

_____

_____

5. Where does Percy watch other people skateboarding?

_____

_____

6. What does he feel when he watches them? _____

_____

_____

_____

TURN the page to start writing Percy's story.

✓ Check It!

Page 73

Suggestions:
1. Percy is 12 years old.
2. He has red hair, green eyes, and freckles. His two front teeth are crooked.
3. Percy lives in a suburban neighborhood called Ditmore Heights. The houses are small but separate, with tiny gardens in front.
4. Percy's idol is Vin Kelleher, an older boy who skateboards in the local park every day. All the kids worship him.
5. There's a skateboard park at the end of Percy's street.
6. When Percy watches Vin skateboard, he feels like that's the one thing in the world that makes a boy look cool. If you want anyone to like you, you need to be a skateboard genius.

Page 74

Suggestion:
Percy Stanton is a 12-year-old boy who lives in suburban Ditmore Heights. He has red hair, green eyes, and a bunch of freckles on his nose. There is a skateboard park at the end of his street, and that's where Percy's idol, Vin Kelleher, skates every day. Vin is amazing. He can do anything on a skateboard.

When Percy watches Vin skate, he smiles a little, so that his two crooked front teeth show. Percy wishes he could skate like Vin. Then he would be as cool as Vin, be as grown up as Vin, and have as many friends as Vin. More than anything else in the world, Percy wants to learn to ride a skateboard.

Page 75

Suggestions:
1. Percy's mom is a worrywart.
2. Percy's mom won't let him have a skateboard because she worries that he'll fall off and hurt himself.
3. When Percy's mom thinks about him learning to skateboard, she gets very, very scared. Being scared makes her act angry.

Percy's mom is a worrier. She especially worries about Percy. She worries that he'll be hit by a car if he plays in the street. She worries that he'll be abducted by strangers if he plays in the front yard. She worries he'll be hit by lightning if he plays in the rain. Most of all, she worries that if he gets a skateboard, he'll fall off and get hurt, so she won't let Percy have a skateboard. Whenever he asks her for one, she gets scared and yells at him: "No! Stop asking, Percy. I mean it!"

✓ Check It!

Page 76

Suggestions:

1. Percy could:
   • borrow a friend's skateboard
   • save up and buy a skateboard
   • convince his mother to let him have one
2. Percy's mom could:
   • take away his friend's skateboard
   • make him return the skateboard he bought
   • forbid Percy to go to the skate park

Page 77

Suggestions:

For the ending, Percy could put his foot down. He could tell his mother that he's twelve years old (or however old you made him), and if he bought a skateboard with his own money, he should be able to keep it and ride it. He could promise that he'll be safe and wear protective gear.

OR: Percy could ask his mother to come with him to the skate park and watch the other kids. Maybe after a little while, she'll feel better about letting Percy ride. They could work out rules for how Percy should be safe.

OR: Percy could give in to his mother and wait to learn to skateboard until he's older.

Page 78

Suggestions:

Percy was angry. His mother didn't have any right to tell him what to buy with his spending money. And he didn't understand why skateboards made her so angry. He took a deep breath and went downstairs to ask her.

She was in the kitchen, banging dishes.

"Mom?" Percy started. "Why are you—"

"I won't listen," Percy's mom said. "I said no and I mean no."

Percy waited for a minute. He took another deep breath. Then he said, "Mom, I'm 12 years old now. I saved up my money to buy that skateboard, and I'm keeping it. I wish you would tell me why it makes you so angry. But I'm going to learn to ride it, no matter what."

Percy's mom started to cry, and Percy felt badly. Finally she told him why she was afraid. She reminded Percy that his father had been a daredevil. He rode a motorcycle and used to jump out of airplanes for fun. Then one day, he had an accident.

"I don't want you to get hurt and leave me all alone!" his mother sobbed.

Percy hugged his mother and promised her that he wouldn't get hurt. He'd be careful and wear pads and a helmet.

"I'll be around for a long time, Ma," he told her. "We're a team."

The next day, he took his new skateboard to the park and asked Vin for a lesson.

WRITE two paragraphs to introduce Percy, his setting, and what he wants most in the world.

_____

_____

_____

_____

_____

_____

_____

_____

_____

_____

_____

_____

_____

_____

_____

_____

_____

_____

_____

_____

_____

_____

Now it's time to introduce Percy's problem.

Problem: Percy's mom won't let him have a skateboard.

FILL IN the blanks.

1. What's Percy's mom like?

_____

_____

2. Why won't Percy's mom let him have a skateboard?

_____

_____

3. How does Percy's mom feel when she thinks about Percy learning to skateboard?

_____

_____

WRITE one paragraph introducing Percy's problem.

_____

_____

_____

_____

_____

_____

_____

How can Percy learn to skateboard anyway? Remember, he has to try a couple of times and fail.

1. LIST the ways Percy could try to solve his problem.

_____

_____

_____

_____

2. Now, LIST all the ways Percy's mom could try to stop him.

_____

_____

_____

_____

CIRCLE your favorites and think about how each character feels about what happens.

WRITE two paragraphs about Percy trying to get what he wants and *failing*.

HINT: What does Percy's mom do each time he tries? Or doesn't he tell her?

Drafting

Time to end Percy's struggle. Does Percy finally learn to skateboard? If so, how? What does his mom do about it? Don't forget to show your characters' feelings.

WRITE the ending to Percy's story.

_____

_____

_____

_____

_____

_____

_____

_____

_____

_____

_____

_____

_____

_____

You did it! That's a draft.

Author! Author!

Time to WRITE a draft of your own story.

HINTS:
1. Check your fiction story map on page 56.
2. Use your plot map from page 64.
3. Reread your sense map from page 68.
4. Don't forget the dialogue.

TURN the page for more space to write.

Drafting

A first draft is never the last. Read it over and look for ways to REVISE it. That means you cut, add, or change things to make your story stronger.

READ this story.

All That Jazz

Jazz is all-American music. It was invented in the United States. While other musicians play from sheet music that tells them which notes to play, jazz musicians *improvise*. That means they make up notes as they go along, so they play the songs differently each time. Jazz players never play a song the same way twice.

Another thing that makes jazz special is its rhythm. Jazz music uses *syncopation*, which is when a song hits an unexpected beat. Instead of BAH-buh-BAH-buh-BAH-buh, a jazz song might go buh-BAH-BAH-buh-buh-BAH. That's not the type of rhythm you'll hear in classical music. It's not used in many older kinds of music. Even though jazz music has been around long enough to be considered classical, it still sounds fresh and new.

This story is too long. CROSS OUT **three** sentences that aren't necessary.

HINT: Why say the same thing twice?

Rereading & Revising

Page 85

Suggestion:

The sharp smell of nail polish told Eli that his sister Marcella was in her room, painting her nails. He threw open her door and grabbed her by the arm.

"You've got to come downstairs!" he cried.

She pulled back. "What are you doing? You'll wreck my primary coat!"

Eli ignored her and dragged her down the stairs. His heart was pounding and he was breathing hard, so it was difficult to talk, but he tried anyway.

"There's a big thing in the backyard," he gasped. "It just landed."

"What kind of big thing?" Marcella asked. They were stumbling by the family photos in the front hallway, and she knocked one off the wall as they passed.

"It's a big spaceship kind of thing," Eli answered as they went through the kitchen.

"A what?" Marcella tried to wrench her arm out of her brother's grip. "Stop fooling around! Why do you have to be such a—"

By this time, they were in the backyard, and she could see for herself.

Page 86

Suggestion:

What else could Olivia try instead of flour?
She could use baking powder. What would that taste like?
She could use face powder. What would that smell like?

OR:

Where could Olivia look for flour?
She could go to the store. How would she get there?
She could ask a neighbor. Are her neighbors weird?

When you're revising your nonfiction story, make sure that your main idea is crystal clear.

READ this story.

Extreme Chocolate Lovers

Some people like baths filled with smelly oils or goopy mud. Why not add chocolate? At the Hotel Hershey in Hershey, Pennsylvania, you can pay $40 to splash around in whipped cocoa for 15 minutes. But can you really get clean in a chocolate bath? Please, don't drink the bath water when you get out. You can also spend $120 on an hour-long cocoa rubdown to relax your muscles. Maybe you'd prefer a chocolate sugar scrub for $65? Don't worry, you can have all this "choco-therapy" without gaining a pound!

The main idea of this story is extreme chocolate lovers. REVISE the story so that the main idea is clear.

HINTS: Rewrite the topic sentence. Cut and rearrange the rest.

_____

_____

_____

_____

_____

_____

_____

_____

Is your story fun to read? Make sure every sentence starts in a different way, and don't repeat the same words all the time.

READ this story.

Pink Flamingoes

Flamingoes are like birds from fantasyland. They're a pink-orange color and have long legs, a long neck, and a bill that turns down at the tip. They almost always stand on one leg with the other leg tucked underneath. They look like they're going to fall over, but they don't. Who knows why they stand that way? Maybe that's how they keep warm. Maybe that's how they keep at least one foot dry all the time since they stand in water a lot. Flamingoes are an unsolved mystery.

REVISE this story so that you're not repeating words and sentence starters.

HINTS: Use some transitions from page 36. It's okay to combine two sentences into one.

_____

_____

_____

_____

_____

_____

_____

_____

_____

Rereading & Revising

Have a friend read your fiction story. Does the main character feel like a real person to your reader? If not, you may need to add more detail.

READ this paragraph.

Plucky Princess

Princess Ballia hated being a princess. She thought it was terrible. So one day, she hid in the back of a cart and escaped into the outside world. Luckily she wasn't caught.

REVISE this paragraph so that the main character is more real.

HINT: Add detail to introduce your reader to Princess Ballia. What does she look like? Why does she hate being a princess? How did she get the idea (and courage) to escape?

_____

_____

_____

_____

_____

_____

_____

_____

_____

_____

_____

Description and dialogue make you *show* a scene rather than just *tell* about it.

READ this paragraph.

Aliens at Eli's House

Eli ran into the house. He found his sister Marcella in her room, painting her nails. He told her he needed her help—fast! As they ran down the stairs, he explained what had happened in the backyard. She didn't believe him until she saw it for herself—an alien spaceship had landed right in Mom's flower beds!

REVISE this scene to make it *show* rather than *tell*.

HINT: Add dialogue, and use your five senses to describe where the characters are and how they feel.

_____

_____

_____

_____

_____

_____

_____

_____

_____

_____

_____

Rereading & Revising

When you reread your fiction story, pay attention to the ending. Does it come too fast?

READ this story.

Olivia's Big Mistake

"I'm going to bake a cake," Olivia announced one day when her parents were away.

First, Olivia put all of the ingredients on the kitchen table. She couldn't find any flour, so she used salt instead.

"Nobody will notice the difference," she said.

After dinner that night, Olivia served her cake. Her family spit it out.

"I guess you noticed the difference," Olivia said sadly.

REVISE the ending of this story so that it doesn't come so quickly.

HINT: Did Olivia try hard enough to solve her problem?

_____

_____

_____

_____

_____

_____

_____

_____

_____

_____

Author! Author!

REREAD and REVISE your nonfiction story draft from page 39. WRITE the revised version here.

_____

_____

_____

_____

_____

_____

_____

_____

_____

_____

_____

_____

_____

_____

_____

_____

_____

_____

_____

_____

_____

_____

TURN the page to finish revising your story.

Proofreading & Editing

12

The final step to a finished story is PROOFREADING. That's when you carefully check for mistakes in spelling, punctuation, and grammar. Then you EDIT the mistakes by fixing them.

READ this story.

I Scream for Ice Cream

I love ice cream. I also happin to be a total expert on the suject. Trust me—during my thirten years on this planet, I've tried it all: forzen custard, frozen yogurt, sorbet, and gelato. But plain old icecream will always reign supreem with me. When it comes to flavors, I like to mix it up a little. Give me plain old vanilla, but top it off with choclate sauce, or buttsercortch, or razzberry syrup. And don't forget teh whipped cream!

CIRCLE the 10 spelling errors in the story.

HINT: Use a dictionary to check words you don't know. WRITE the correct words in the blanks.

1. _____
2. _____
3. _____
4. _____
5. _____
6. _____
7. _____
8. _____
9. _____
10. _____

✓ Check It!

Page 89

1. happen
2. subject
3. thirteen
4. frozen
5. ice cream
6. supreme
7. chocolate
8. butterscotch
9. raspberry
10. the

Page 91

Connor's Sick Day

One morning, Connor decided to be sick, so he stayed in bed.

"Connor, time for school," his dad said.

Connor just groaned.

A few minutes later, Connor's mom came to get him.

"Connor, time for school," she said.

"I don't feel well," Connor said. He tried to look very sick.

It worked! Connor stayed home while his parents went to work. First, he watched TV, but there wasn't anything good on. Next, he made himself a sandwich out of peanut butter, chocolate sauce, and marshmallows. Then, he played video games for three hours. Finally, he made a milkshake with strawberries, frozen yogurt, lemon-lime soda, and butterscotch.

When his parents came home from work, Connor was back in bed.

"Do you feel better, honey?" his mom asked.

Connor groaned and grabbed his stomach. "No, I feel much worse."

89

Proofreading & Editing

When you proofread your story, you can use special proofreading marks to flag the mistakes. Then you can find them and fix them.

Page 92

"Howdy, Ajax!" cried Bambo.
"Yo, Bambo," said Ajax. He sighed.
"What's wrong?" Bambo asked.
Ajax said, "Everything's wrong today."
"Well," said Bambo. "What's the worst thing?"
Ajax thought for a minute. "It's the first thing in the morning," he said.

∧ When something's missing you can add it this mark. *using*

⊙ Use this mark to add a period⊙

≡ did you forget to capitalize a letter? use this mark.

/ To Make a letter lowercase instead, uSe this Mark.

℘ To to cut something, use that mark.

¶ Want to make a new paragraph? Use this mark. *this ¶*

PROOFREAD this story, using proofreading marks.

HINT: Watch the verb tenses.

Connor's Sick Day

One morning, Connor decided to be sick,

so he stayed in bed.

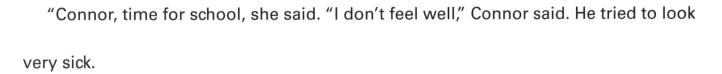

"connor, time for school," his dad Said.

Connor just groaned

A few minurtes later, Connors mom came to get him.

"Connor, time for school, she said. "I don't feel well," Connor said. He tried to look

very sick.

It worked! Connor stayed hoMe while his parents to work.

first, he watchd TV, but there wasn't anything good on. Next, he made himself a

sandwich out of peanut butter chocolate sauce, and marshmalows. Then, he play

video video games for three hours Finally, he made a Milkshake with strawberries,

frozen yogurt lemon-lime soda, and butterscotch.

When his parents are came home from work, Connor was back in Bed.

"Do you feel better, honey" his mom asked.

Connor groan and grabbed his stomach. "No, I feel much worse."

Proofreading & Editing

Dialogue can be tricky. You need to make sure the quotation marks and punctuation are in the right place. Look inside any fiction book to see how it works.

Here's the RIGHT way to do it.

"How's my hair?" asked John.

"I think it looks great," said Annie.

"I don't know." John shook his head.

"Maybe it's too fluffy."

Annie replied, "Fluffy is cute."

"Yuck!" John ran out of the room to wet his head again.

PROOFREAD this dialogue, using proofreading marks.

"Howdy, Ajax" cried Bambo!

"Yo, Bambo. said Ajax. He sighed."

"What's wrong," Bambo asked? Ajax said "everything's wrong today."

"Well" said Bambo "What's the worst thing?" Ajax thought for a minute.

It'sthe first thing in the morning, he said.

Now, EDIT it. That means REWRITE the dialogue so that all the errors are fixed.

_____

_____

_____

_____

_____

_____

_____

Author! Author!

It's time to polish your own work. First, proofread and edit your nonfiction story from pages 87 and 88. Then, WRITE the final draft here.

_____

_____

_____

_____

_____

_____

_____

_____

_____

_____

_____

_____

_____

_____

_____

_____

_____

_____

_____

TURN the page to finish your final draft.

Author! Author!

Now, revise, proofread, and edit your fiction story from pages 79 and 80.
WRITE the final draft here.

_____

_____

_____

_____

_____

_____

_____

_____

_____

_____

_____

_____

_____

_____

_____

_____

_____

_____

TURN the page to finish your final draft.

When you share your story with the world, you PUBLISH it. You already know lots of ways to publish a story.

✓ Check It!

Page 97

Suggestions:

1. Print:
- magazines
- books
- newspapers

2. Film or TV:
- sitcoms
- movies
- newscasts
- documentaries

3. Internet:
- online videos
- Web sites
- online news magazines

4. Live performance:
- plays
- read alouds
- radio news shows

1. LIST three ways stories are published in PRINT.

comic books

2. LIST three ways stories are published on FILM or TV.

cartoons

3. LIST three ways stories are published on the INTERNET.

online journals (blogs)

4. LIST three ways stories are PERFORMED live.

puppet shows

Author! Author!

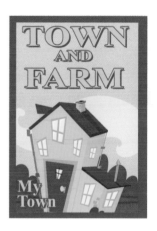

WRITE a paragraph about your town for a national magazine read by grownups.

An e-mail you send to your best buddy is going to sound a lot different than a letter you write to your grandma, right? You should always remember your readers when you're writing or publishing a story.

_____

_____

_____

_____

_____

_____

_____

_____

_____

_____

_____

_____

_____

_____

_____

_____

This time, WRITE a paragraph about your town for a local kids Web site. What will be different?

Publishing

LIST places where you could publish your nonfiction story from pages 93 and 94.

_____

_____

_____

_____

_____

_____

_____

LIST places where you could publish your fiction story from pages 95 and 96.

_____

_____

_____

_____

_____

_____

_____

Now you know where to start. Good luck!

Now you know it all, right? Prove it!

Let's start with an argument.

Topic: Kids having jobs

Opinion: _____

_____

Facts: _____

_____

_____

_____

Do you need a call to action?

If so, WRITE it here. _____

_____

_____

Now, TURN the page to WRITE your argument.

HINTS:

1. START with your opinion as the topic sentence.
2. SUPPORT your opinion with facts from the fact list.
3. END by stating your goal and call to action.

Author! Author!

WRITE your argument about kids having jobs, using the map on the previous page.

_____

_____

_____

_____

_____

_____

_____

_____

_____

_____

_____

_____

_____

_____

_____

_____

_____

_____

Now, REREAD and REVISE your argument.

HINTS:
1. Is your opinion stated clearly?
2. Do all your sentences start differently?
3. How many facts do you use to support your argument?
4. Don't forget to cut sentences you don't need.

_____

_____

_____

_____

_____

_____

_____

_____

_____

_____

_____

_____

_____

_____

_____

_____

_____

Nonfiction Review

Time to write a nonfiction story.

First, PICK a genre. _____

HINT: See some choices on pages 2 through 5.

Next, PICK a topic.

Big Topic: _____

Smaller Topics:

_____

_____

_____

CIRCLE the topic you want to write about.

WRITE your topic sentence. _____

_____

_____

LIST all the facts you know about this topic.

HINT: Don't forget to research if you need to.

_____

_____

_____

_____

_____

FILL IN this story map, using the facts from the previous page.

Topic:

Topic Sentence:

_____

_____

Paragraph 1. Main Idea

_____

_____

Supporting Details

1. _____

2. _____

3. _____

Paragraph 2. Main Idea

_____

_____

Supporting Details

1. _____

2. _____

3. _____

Paragraph 3. Main Idea

_____

_____

Supporting Details

1. _____

2. _____

3. _____

Paragraph 4. Main Idea

_____

_____

Supporting Details

1. _____

2. _____

3. _____

Author! Author!

Now you've got what it takes! WRITE your first draft of this new nonfiction story. Use the map on page 105.

HINTS:

1. Write the details into sentences.
2. Combine the sentences into main idea paragraphs.
3. Make the paragraphs flow into each other.
4. End with your conclusion (or your call to action).

_____

_____

_____

_____

_____

_____

_____

_____

_____

_____

_____

_____

_____

_____

TURN the page to start your final draft.

Now, REREAD your story draft.

FILL IN the blanks to come up with a plan for revision.

1. Is your topic sentence boring or unclear? WRITE another version here.

   _____

   _____

2. Do each of your paragraphs have a main idea? LIST them.

   Paragraph 1 Main Idea: _____

   Paragraph 2 Main Idea: _____

   Paragraph 3 Main Idea: _____

   Paragraph 4 Main Idea: _____

3. Do all your sentences start differently? Are you using transitions? UNDERLINE any sentences that need to be rewritten.

4. Does your story end with a strong conclusion or call to action? WRITE a strong ending sentence here.

   _____

   _____

5. Are all of your facts correct? RESEARCH one new fact and WRITE it here.

   _____

   _____

Now you're ready to revise.

Author! Author!

REVISE your nonfiction story, using your notes from the previous page.

_____

_____

_____

_____

_____

_____

_____

_____

_____

_____

_____

_____

_____

_____

_____

_____

_____

_____

_____

_____

_____

_____

_____

_____

_____

TURN the page to finish your final draft.

You've written one fiction story. It's time for another.

First, PICK a genre. _____

FILL IN the blanks with some character ideas.

_____ is a _____ who
NAME   TYPE

_____.
                                    WANTS

FILL IN the blanks with some setting ideas.

_____ is a _____ that's
NAME   TYPE

_____.
                                DESCRIPTION

FILL IN the blanks with some problem ideas.

_____

_____

_____

_____

Now, FILL IN this story map.

Main Character(s)

_____

_____

_____

_____

_____

Problem

_____

_____

_____

_____

_____

Title

_____

Solution

_____

_____

_____

_____

Setting

_____

_____

_____

_____

_____

How will your main character get what he or she wants?

FILL IN this plot map.

Title _____

The first thing that happens is _____

_____

The problem _____

_____

After that _____

_____

After that _____

_____

The solution _____

_____

_____

Fiction Review

PICK a person, place, or thing from your story.

FILL IN this sense map with ways to describe it.

Topic:

Get to know your main character better. FILL IN the blanks.

How old is your main character? _____

What does he or she look like?

_____

_____

Where does he or she live?

_____

_____

What is his or her favorite thing to do?

_____

_____

Why does your character want what he or she wants?

_____

_____

What's stopping your character from getting it?

_____

_____

If there's a person standing in the way, what is this person's problem?

_____

_____

Author! Author!

You've done all the steps. Now WRITE a draft of this new fiction story.

TURN the page to finish your final draft.

Fiction Review

Now, REREAD your story draft. FILL IN the blanks to come up with a plan for revision.

1. Does your main character seem like a real person with real feelings? WRITE one more character detail that you could include in your story.

   _____

   _____

2. Is it clear what your character wants? UNDERLINE where you wrote about it in the story.

3. CIRCLE any paragraphs that could use dialogue.

4. LIST three people, places, or things that you could describe better.

   _____

   _____

   _____

5. Did your character try hard enough to get what he or she wants? WRITE one more way he or she could try, and what happens.

   _____

   _____

   _____

   _____

REVISE your fiction story, using your notes from the previous page.

_____

_____

_____

_____

_____

_____

_____

_____

_____

_____

_____

_____

_____

_____

_____

_____

_____

_____

_____

_____

_____

_____

_____

_____

TURN the page to finish your final draft.

Fiction Review

You really know your stuff. Someday the whole world might be reading your big ideas. So keep writing!